Building My Life

Building My Life

An Autobiography

Pat Franchi

Copyright © 2014 by Pat Franchi
All Rights Reserved

This is an autobiography.

Without limiting the rights under copyright reserved above,
no part of this publication may be reproduced,
stored in or introduced into a retrieval system,
or transmitted, in any form or by any means
(electronic, mechanical, photocopying, recording or otherwise),
without the prior written permission of the copyright owner.

The author wishes to acknowledge Wikipedia,
as a source for checking dates, common facts and proper spelling.

First Edition
2014

Printed in the United States of America

ISBN-13: 978-1494254933
ISBN-10: 149425493X

For My Family

*I would like to acknowledge my appreciation
to my Father and Mother—
and for all of my family and friends—
for their support, friendship and love.
They have enriched my life.*

Contents

Chapter One: Gallinaro 1
Chapter Two: California and Nevada Streets 17
Chapter Three: Semper Fi 25
Chapter Four: A Real Lunch 29
Chapter Five: On Our Own 32
Chapter Six: Madeline..42
Chapter Seven: I Had a Vision 49
Chapter Eight: Land 54
Chapter Nine: Bella Luna..60
Chapter Ten: Over There 67
Chapter Eleven: Famiglia..77
Chapter Twelve: The Light Fails...80
Chapter Thirteen: With Six, You Coach Little League..............86
Chapter Fourteen: To the Slopes—and Beyond 88
Chapter Fifteen: Goals 94
Chapter Sixteen: Tradition 97
    Photographs..106
Chapter Seventeen: My Kids 146
Chapter Eighteen: Christmas Carols 160
Chapter Nineteen: New and Old Chapters 164
Chapter Twenty: Back to the Land..167
Chapter Twenty-One: Money..179
Chapter Twenty-Two: Bocce—and Those Other Sports 182
Chapter Twenty-Three: Fran 198
Chapter Twenty-Four: Yahoo! This is Fun!............................213
Chapter Twenty-Five: Grandpa 217
Chapter Twenty-Six: The Long Way Home............................221
Chapter Twenty-Seven: What Do We Build?.........................224

BUILDING MY LIFE

CHAPTER ONE
Gallinaro

I never look back. I always look forward. Why dwell on past mistakes? Why dwell on sad memories? You can't change any of it. All you can do is look forward and do your best to do the right thing. You can learn from your past. But there's no point in dwelling on the past. It robs you of energy. And you need all of your energy for the job ahead.

That's the way I've built my business. But, much more importantly, it's the way I've built my family. It's the way I've built my life.

Of course, to tell you my story, I have to look back a little. At least to the beginning.

I was born next to a fireplace, on a concrete floor.

January 31, 1928.

Gallinaro, Italy.

My parents were Luigi and Giovanna Franchi.

They lived in Gallinaro in a stone farmhouse. It was a very rustic house, the kind you'd see on old postcards or in movies about Italy before World War II.

Gallinaro is in central Italy, in the Lazio region, in the province of Frosinore. It is about seventy miles east of Rome, near Monte Casino. It's rich farming land, and, of course, it's great land for vineyards and fruit groves. It's peasant land. The backbone of Italy. My family worked the land and grew wheat and grapes, and they had fruit trees as well as corn and other crops—but wheat and grapes were the main products.

Pane e vino.

I told you it was the backbone of Italy.

There is an interesting wrinkle to this story—about how I came to be born and about how my family came to live in America. Well, maybe more than one wrinkle.

Let's start with the house in Gallinaro. It was built by my grandparents, my father's parents, Dominico Antonio and Pasqua Franchi. They had six sons and one daughter: Leonardo, Pasquale, Carmile, Gioseppi, Carmen, Luigi (my father) and Angelina.

Let me point out that my grandmother Pasqua had twenty-one children—but only seven survived.

Well, my father, Luigi, married a wonderful young woman, Giovanna, who was just sixteen. They were to have four sons and one daughter.

But, before any of their children were born, a few things had happened. My father's parents both passed away. Then my father's oldest brother, my Uncle Gioseppi, left Italy and came to live in America, in Newton, Massachusetts. Three more of my father's brothers—Leonardo, Pasquale and Carmile—were also out of the house and living on their own. And my father's sister, my Aunt Angelina, had married and moved with her husband into her own house in Gallinaro.

This left my father and and my mother Giovanna, as well as my father's brother, Carmen, and his wife Filomena, living in the homestead in Gallinaro.

Okay. So two families were in our house when I was growing up.

We lived in separate sections, almost like separate apartments. But the families were all under the same roof—parents and kids—living and eating and working together. As the story goes, my father and mother, apparently, had the better section to live in.

The house was made entirely of stone and concrete and was very solid. But—typical of the day—there was no electricity and there was no indoor plumbing. We used candles and lamps for light; and we used an outhouse.

Everyone we knew lived that way, so we didn't take any particular notice of it.

One improvement my father made, right after he got married, was to build a new well. It was huge by local standards: fifty-to-sixty-feet deep and twelve-feet wide.

The well was to be located thirty feet from my mother's kitchen—to make her life easier. My father had to dig the well entirely by hand, using a pick and shovel. There were no retaining walls to hold the dirt back as he dug. It could have collapsed and buried him.

But he did it. He dug it all out and he lined the entire well with rocks that he and my mother had to carry from a mountain that was a half mile away. To move the rocks, he used a cart pulled by cattle. There were no power tools or tractors or trucks.

But, because of the new well, there *was* an abundant supply of water at all times! In fact, during dry seasons, many neighbors would come by with buckets to borrow water.

I've been back to visit the house—and the well still works! The water still tastes as sweet.

My father then decided that he wanted to own the house outright. To do that, he had to buy out his brothers. And to do that, he needed to make money.

To make money, he had to go to America.

An odd sort of pattern developed.

My father would leave Gallinaro and his family—his wife and his two young boys: Gerardo who was three years old and Dominic who was one year old. He'd take a boat to America to live in Massachusetts with his older brother Gioseppi and work on construction jobs. They also collected coal from the railroad tracks and would sell it to homeowners for heating or cooking purposes. In this way my father was able to live and to save money.

In fact, he'd save up a sizable amount of money and then—every five years or so—he would return to Italy for a visit. He'd use the money he'd made in the States to make payments to his brothers for the land and the house that he wanted to own. The plan was working.

When my father came for his next visit—and his next payment to his brothers—he and my mother, as the story goes, had decided that they didn't want more children for a while. So the visit was somewhat uneventful.

As fate would have it—as fate usually has it—my father said goodbye to my mother and his two sons, Gerardo and Dominic, and went to Naples to take the ship back to America.

But the boat wasn't going anywhere. Something "broke," as my father would say, and the trip was postponed.

My father, naturally, returned to Gallinaro and extended his visit.

He managed to extend his family as well, because, when the boat was "fixed" and he set sail, he left Giovanna at home on the farm—pregnant once again. She soon gave birth to me. They named me Pasquale, after my Uncle Pasquale who had died very young from a heart attack—he had been the sheriff of Gallinaro. I've always been called Pat.

Then, apparently, all plans were thrown out the window, because my father made two more visits home and each time he left my mother pregnant; my sister Maria was born next and then my younger brother Tony.

Well, my mother finally reached the point where she had had it with this system. Her husband would leave. Come back. She'd get pregnant. Her husband would leave again.

Apparently, a day came when she said something like, "Enough is enough."

America or Italy.

One or the other.

My father chose Italy. On what he thought would be his last trip to America, he bought a lot of tools. Tools he would need to run the farm and the vineyard. He had them all shipped to our house in Gallinaro.

When he came back to Gallinaro, the tools were waiting for him and he got to work.

The first thing he did was to finish buying out his brothers. So now he—we—owned the house and all the land outright. My father's brother and family still lived in the house, but my father owned it.

My father was happy. My mother was happy. We were working the land and doing very well.

It was a simple life. We would work during the day; it was hard work, but it made us feel good. At night after dinner—always a good dinner—we'd sit by the fireplace and talk and discuss the farm and the world and everything in between.

In cold weather, we'd heat bricks in the fireplace and take them to bed and put them under the covers for heat. There was no heat in the house at all, except for that one large fireplace.

Besides the house, we also had a barn, where we kept cows, horses, pigs and sheep. We also had a chicken coop, where we raised chickens so that we could sell the eggs—and have chicken for dinner on a special occasion.

In our fields, we grew a lot of different crops: wheat, corn, grapes, olives, figs and just about anything else we needed. The only things we ever bought at the markets in town were clothes and tools—and things like salt and pepper. And oranges! Pretty much everything we needed, we had on the farm.

We also had a few pigs on the farm—and they were almost my undoing! What happened was that my brother Dominic was supposed to be taking care of me during the day while my mother and my older brother Jerry worked in the fields. Dominic was about seven and I was about six months old.

Now, in those days, infants were bundled up tightly. Wrapped all around, like a mummy. The idea was that the tight wrapping would make your bones stronger and make your spine very straight.

On that day, Dominic wasn't paying attention to me. I was wrapped like a mummy and couldn't move or go anywhere. Or so he thought.

A pig—one of our pigs—came along and picked me up by my wrappings with his mouth! And then the pig took off! With me!

Dominic and my mother chased after the pig and were able to rescue me. But Dominic was not happy after my mother was done with him! He never took his eyes off me again.

My mother had to be in control. She had so much work to do—plus raising a family—that she had to delegate things. We all had to pitch in and help. She had to be able to rely on us. And, of course, no one wants a pig to come and take the baby!

My mother was a workhorse. There's no other way to say it.

For instance, when the corn was harvested, she and we kids and a few hired helpers would carry all the corn in baskets to a concrete-floor patio area that was outside the house—and we would make a huge pile of corn. Then we'd start shucking it. I remember that they made a party out of it. They sang and joked and treated it almost like a fun thing to do, even though it was work.

When all the corn was shucked, my mother brought in a rented machine, and they used it to strip all the kernels of corn off of the cobs.

They did the same thing with wheat. Out in the field, they'd cut the wheat by hand and make large bundles out of it. They'd let it sit for days until it was dry and then they'd put several bundles on their heads and take it to the patio. My mother hired a threshing machine to separate the wheat from the chaff.

Once the corn and the wheat were shucked and threshed—leaving only the kernels—it would all be stored in what we called the vault—a large wood chamber. When needed, sacks of corn or wheat would be taken into town to a mill, where it would be ground into meal, and then it would be made into bread or pasta or it would be sold. With the money from selling corn and wheat, my mother would buy seeds for the next year's crops or use the money to pay bills or buy cloth or other things we needed that we didn't produce ourselves.

We also grew grapes. We used some of the grapes for making wine and sold the extra grapes to other people who had small grape vineyards.

It was a lot of work, but, again, we all made a beautiful time out of it. They called the annual event, "La Cantina"—which means "bar," but, in this case, more-or-less meant "fiesta."

All the grapes were dumped into a big concrete tub—just like in the movies. And someone would get inside the tub, with shoes off of course, and stomp on the grapes. The ladies who harvested the grapes for my mother would walk up to the tub, carrying the grapes in baskets on their heads, and dump the grapes into the tub.

I was often one of the "stompers." It was hard work, but it was a lot of fun too.

All the juice from the grapes was put into barrels—really large barrels that I could stand inside of—and was then fermented into wine.

My mother made white and red wine.

We'd all drink it. Even at an early age. But you have to realize that the wine we kids drank was wine that my mother made with a very low alcohol content. She cut the fermenting time way down. That wine was just for the kids. It was, when you come down to it, all natural—no added sugar or anything. I grew up on it. We drank it at meals instead of water.

We really only used water to cook with and to wash our feet!

When it came to making olive oil, I had a major role, in part because I was small. My job was to climb the olive trees and shake the branches. The olives would fall to the ground and land in a sheet we had spread out. Then we'd take them to a nearby mill where the olives were crushed into olive oil.

Our animals provided all of our meat. Every fall, for instance, my mother would butcher one or two pigs and we'd end up with pork chops and sausages and bacon and prosciutto. I wonder if that was the fate of "my" pig.

It wasn't all fun. It wasn't all idyllic.

As I said, one of my father's brothers—my Uncle Carmen—lived in the house with his wife Filomena. Carmen, well, he drank a lot of wine. He had a temper when he drank and he often argued with his wife.

One night, a really bad night, my Uncle Carmen was berating his wife. I was young so I don't remember it exactly. He may have hit her. He certainly had often been rough with her.

Another brother, my Uncle Leonardo who was visiting, was fed up with these episodes. He got up and yelled at his brother and said he was sick and tired of the way his brother had been treating his wife all of these past years.

Threats were made by Carmen. He had a gun—a double-barreled hunting rifle. Leonardo jumped up and grabbed the gun. He screamed at Carmen that enough was enough and that he wasn't going to let Carmen threaten Filomena again. Leonardo took the gun and smashed it against the wall so that Carmen could never use it again. But,

Leonardo didn't know that the gun was loaded and when he hit it against the wall it went off—and the bullet killed him.

The police came of course. My abusive uncle was arrested and charged with what we would now call domestic violence. He ended up in prison, where he died. I never saw him again.

In one night—in one moment—we lost two uncles. My father lost two of his brothers.

You think about these things and wonder what could have happened differently? How life could have been different if that one argument hadn't happened. On the other hand, what would life have been like for my poor aunt?

These are things that you just can't waste energy on. You have to move on.

Indeed, life in Gallinaro went on. My father made trip after trip. My mother had children and worked and worked and worked.

I remember one scary day. My mother and two of my brothers were plowing a field. We didn't have any machinery, we didn't have a tractor. My mother used a big iron plow pulled by cattle.

They were at the field, which was quite far from the house. And it started to rain. It rained really hard. My mother and brothers put the plows in the cart and harnessed the cattle to the cart and started the long wet ride home. But the roads were dirt roads and everything was turning to mud.

They came up to a sharp curve, with a river rushing by on one side.

The cart slid on the mud and slid off the road and went right into the river, with the cows still attached to the harnesses. Without hesitating, my mother and brothers jumped into the river and fought the current and the rain and the animals and somehow managed to free the cows and get them out.

In the midst of it all, my mother cried out to Saint Anthony for help.

San Antonio!

They made it out. People. Cows. No one was hurt.

When my younger brother was born, my mother named him Antonio—in thanks to the saint for helping her save every person and animal. She thought it was a miracle that no one was hurt.

Speaking of miracles, my mother was a very hard worker—she was a very realistic person. She was also very, very religious. She prayed a lot in the evenings and went to church on Sundays and many other days as well. She was devoted to a number of saints—and never missed commemorating their feast days.

I remember when I was young, maybe seven or eight years old, I was having a problem with my left eye. It was swollen; it was bulging out and it really hurt quite a bit. So my mother took me to see a doctor and was told that I had a large tumor behind the eye which was pushing the eyeball out of the socket, and they had to operate and remove the eye. My mother started to cry. We went home and then she took me to a second doctor. He said the same thing. The tumor had to be removed and the only way to do it was to remove the eye. I would lose the eye, but it had to be done.

My mother broke down and cried again. Then we went to a third doctor—with the same results.

She had no choice but to agree to the operation, and a date was set for it. This meant I would lose my left eye.

My mother, being so religious, pleaded with Saint Rocco for help. In the Catholic church, Saint Rocco is the patron saint of protection against the plague and all contagious diseases. I didn't know it at the time, but Saint Rocco is a highly venerated saint in Italy.

My mother promised that if he saved my eye, she would make special devotion to him. She promised that on his feast day she would walk barefoot to his church—which was five-to-six miles from our house. She also promised that she would kneel inside the back of the church and then walk on her knees all the way to the front, to the altar.

If only he would grant her the miracle of curing my eye.

Now—think what you will—but on the day for my surgery we went to the hospital and when the doctor examined me he saw that the tumor had disappeared. It was gone. The bulging was gone. The pain was gone.

There was no longer a reason to operate.

The doctor couldn't understand what had taken place. But my mother knew. Saint Rocco had performed a miaracle and that was all there was to it.

I remember very well that my mother fulfilled her promise.

The church was in the village of Casalvieri—which was, like I said, about five miles away. On August 16, Saint Rocco's feast day, she took me by the hand and we walked to Casalvieri. She was barefoot and her feet were bleeding before long. She continued all the way to the church. At the entrance, as she had promised, she fell to her knees and walked on her knees—not crawling, but walking on her knees—all the way up the long aisle to the altar. She prayed to Saint Rocco to thank him for saving my eye.

That was a long time ago in a faraway land.

I believe it was a miracle, granted to me through my mother. I believe that due to her—because she was so religious—I kept my eye and never had another problem.

Whatever it means to you, I know miracles do happen. Have faith.

Let's return to our farm in Gallinaro and all the work that had to be done. You must realize that everything—everything my mother and the family did—had to be done by hand. For example, there were no washing machines. On laundry days, my mother would walk to the river carrying the clothes to be washed in a large basket on her head. I went along, but all I did was play in the water while my mother washed the clothes on large rocks. She made it look like it was fun; and she would meet other women there and they would have a chance to converse.

Women had a hard time.

When we came to America, my mother took one look around and said, "I will never go back!"

Except of course for vacations.

She enjoyed her life in America.

She saw herself as the boss—and why not? After all that she had gone through in Italy, being a single mother most of the time and raising her family and being responsible for the farm, she certainly had earned it.

But—how did we get to America?

Well, once my father decided to stay in Italy and work the farm, they had no intention of leaving.

But then, as is usually the case, something happened.

My father and my mother would go into town from time to time—to go to the market and get whatever they needed for the week.

On one Monday, and I remember this very well, as they were coming home, a really bad storm came. So much rain and wind! Driving rain. Blinding rain. Almost like a hurricane.

They made it home okay.

But in the morning when the sun came up—well, everything was ruined. The wheat in the fields had been flattened. It was destroyed. The entire crop.

And the vineyards were worse!

Everything was knocked down.

That entire crop was also gone.

There would be no harvest.

My father looked over everything. He owned all of it. And all of it was lost.

He looked at us.

He raised his voice. He made a pronouncement.

And when he made a pronouncement—there was no discussion.

No king of Italy or of anywhere else could have commanded more obedience.

He looked at us, and he said, "We're going to America."

And that was that. He checked his passport—which he saw was still good—and he left for America within a few days. As soon as he got here, he started working on the documents to call Gerardo to America, since Gerardo was the first born.

We had a foothold in the New World.

In 1940—just a year before America got attacked at Pearl Harbor and was drawn into World War II—my father got the documents for the rest of the family.

And off we went to Naples—where, believe it or not, I had my first banana!

We boarded the boat for the new land—my mother and my brothers Dominic and Tony and my sister Maria and I.

The lady with the torch welcomed us with her placid smile. We didn't get off at Ellis Island; we docked at a regular wharf in New York Harbor.

So there we were. And there was New York City. We could see the skyscrapers and the teaming city of wonder that they watched over. It was a little bit scary, but also exciting. And, of course, it was challenging—since we didn't know one word of English.

This was not Gallinaro.

It took a while, but we got all of us and all of the luggage off of the boat. My father met us at the docks. It was very emotional to see my father again, and I remember that he gave each of us a candy bar. Then he got us and the luggage into a taxi and off we went to the train station.

Then—again—luggage, children, parents, tickets, seats.

We sat in our seats and looked out the window and then the train began to move. Out of New York, going north and east, up to New England. To a town called Newton, Massachusetts.

We were bound for home, which at first, was 504 California Street, a first-floor apartment with two or three bedrooms and a kitchen. It was somewhat tight, but workable. It was near school and church, which we were able to walk to. And there was shopping nearby, in a village called Silver Lake or Nonantum—which was known as the Italian Village.

Nonantum—which is an Algonquin word that means "peace"—is one of thirteen villages in Newton.

But it really wasn't a village—there were about 5,000 people living there.

Like I said, it was pretty much an Italian enclave. It was hard for "outsiders" to purchase land or homes, because the Italians wanted to stay within themselves.

It wasn't a wealthy village, but it was a very safe place to live.

There was practically no crime.

People stuck together.

It was great for families. It still is today.

BUILDING MY LIFE

CHAPTER TWO
California and Nevada Streets

We settled into the rented house at 504 California Street.

We had electricity and plumbing!

We had indoor toilets!

What a country!

My mother took the kitchen and made it her own. My father went to work in construction again. My older brother Jerry became a baker, and Dominic went to work with my father. My mother and my older brothers went to night school for English. The rest of us did our best to become Americans.

I couldn't speak a word of English, but, as soon as I arrived, I enrolled in the fifth grade of the Carr School—the public school—on Nevada Street.

I should have been in the sixth or seventh grade—but, since I couldn't speak any English, they put me in fifth grade.

It was hard to understand and respond, but I caught on pretty quickly.

There was a boy by the name of Rico Bianchi—who was Italian like me but had arrived a few years earlier and was good at English. They teamed me up with him and he translated. The teacher would send us both out to the hallway so Rico could catch me up on what was going on in class.

I caught on, of course, over time. It goes without saying that my first English word was a cuss word. Anyway, I did pretty well in school. Then I went to junior high. Then I went to Newton Trade School. I became a machinist.

I graduated in 1946, the year after the war ended. My brother Gerardo was in the service during the war. He was a Seabee, and he saw action in the Pacific. He was honorably discharged and returned to live at home until he got married.

Gerardo—let's call him Jerry—and I were very close. I remember times, back in Italy, when I was small and we had to walk someplace far away, that he carried me on his shoulders. Whenever there may have been a problem, or a punishment from my parents, he would always stick by me—and I did the same for him.

After we got to America, and I was attending school, my parents and my two older brothers had full-time jobs. We all had to help pay bills—we all had to pitch in for the good of the family.

My mother worked in a factory right near our house. It was the Ucinite Manufacturing Company and it made electrical systems for the automobile industry. It's amazing when you think of it, that my mother had five children, a house, a garden, livestock—and she worked full time for about forty years too!

She'd leave lots of notes—of errands that had to be run and chores that we had to do after school.

My father, since he was a mason, didn't work during the winter. My mother would leave him a list of chores to do and errands to run every morning before she left for work.

The problem was that my father liked to sleep late. So he had to set an alarm to make sure he'd get up in time to get things done before my mother got home for lunch.

Every day, my mother would come home and make lunch for herself and my father and check on how things were going—and then she'd return to work.

And in the morning, before she left, she still had to make lunches for all of us—especially my twenty sandwiches (I'll talk more about my lunches later)—and make sure all the clothes were ready and the house was clean and food was there for dinner.

I was in school during this time, but I pitched in as well and got a part-time job at the John T. Lodge Wool Factory, working from 4:00 P.M. to 10:00 P.M., Monday through Saturday. I made twenty or thirty cents an hour and was proud to be bringing pay to my dad. That's six hours a day—for six days a week. And we called it "part time."

I'd get up in the morning and go to school, and then I'd go to the factory right after school. I did my homework at the factory during our dinner break.

It was tough work. We'd stand at big tables and take bales of cloth that were in different colors and we'd lay them out and mash them together and then use machines to break the cloth and wool until it was the color that was needed.

All this is the reason that when I eventually joined the Marines it wasn't so tough for me. I was used to long days and hard work.

No one in my family ever doubted what we had to do or resented it in any way. We had a house and land to keep up and pay for. There was no choice really. Through it all, my mother was the driving force. She was the doer of the family, even though my father was the boss.

My mother had the vision of getting ahead and to own our own house. This was because my mother had always lived in a home that we owned and it was hard for her to see us paying rent every month and not getting anything out of it. She felt that the money we were paying for rent should go toward a mortgage.

One Sunday morning she happened to pass by a house on her way to church and she saw a for-sale sign. Well, she didn't rest after that! Not until she convinced my father to buy the house. I had never seen my mother so happy.

This is how we came to live in the house at 281 Nevada Street. That's where we lived during my childhood, and it's still owned today by our family.

We were still in Nonatum Village and still close to Silver Lake, really a pond, where we went ice skating in winter. We could also walk to church and school and markets.

It was a single-family house in an area with a lot of two-family homes.

And it was big, nine rooms with a kitchen, dining room, family room, living room and bathroom on the first floor, and four bedrooms on the second floor.

There was a huge yard in back—a big empty space. So my mother started a garden. She grew everything: tomatoes, beans, carrots, squash—you name it. My mother had a green thumb.

The yard became key to our lives.

My mother had my father build a chicken coop and a rabbit hutch.

My mother put a lot of work into raising chickens and rabbits. She'd sell some of them to neighbors from time to time, and she sold a lot of chicken eggs. We ate a lot of the eggs and the chickens ourselves. We had so much chicken to eat that I really don't care for chicken dinners anymore.

I remember my mother going out and buying 100 to 150 baby chicks in early winter. My father was responsible for them; he initially set them up in the basement and then moved them outside to the coop when they were older.

When they were ready to be butchered, my sister and I would go out in the neighborhood, door to door, selling chickens and vegetables. I had one of those classic Radio Flyer red wagons. I'd put a few chickens and some vegetables in it and we'd knock on doors and ask if anyone wanted to buy them! Imagine kids doing that today?

I was in charge of butchering. I was good at it; I would do it quickly and drain all the blood out of the chicken, which made it better for cooking. I didn't mind this work at all—after all, it's what they were raised for. No one minds buying chicken at a market wrapped in cellophane, so why should anyone mind how the chicken gets there in the first place?

Of course, being a kid, I did try once to kill them with my BB gun. It didn't work at all. That night, we happened to be eating one of those chickens for dinner and all of a sudden my father bit on something hard and then took a BB out of his mouth. He was not pleased with that and it was not a good evening for me.

I also took care of the rabbits—killing and skinning them—but we didn't have that many rabbits.

We did have pigs.

My father bought them from a local farmer and then my father would butcher them as needed, and I was his helper. I was good at that as well. I could cut up all the meat and I knew what parts were used for sausage and ham and chops and proscuitto.

I liked making sausage. We didn't use a machine to grind up the meat; we didn't like the way that tasted. So we would use a knife and cut the meat into little pieces and then use seasonings and stuff the meat into the casings. We made both hot and sweet sausage.

Have you ever had pigs' feet?

I love pigs' feet. I still make them. I go to Stop & Shop and buy them. Then I boil them twice—rinsing in between—to both cook them and to take out all the fat. To the meat you add celery and potatoes and parsley and beans and then cook it all up.

It's elegant. It's a real delicacy. The meat is so tender it just falls off of the bone. One thing about a pig—nothing goes to waste.

We had a wine cellar in the basement and we'd hang all the cut meat down there to dry out.

We did a lot of work. We had to. That's why I think that young kids today should have part-time jobs while they're in school. It makes you appreciate what you have and what things cost and what you have to do to support yourself and your family. We grew up with the understanding of what it took to earn a dollar—and how to best spend it. Kids learn about life from working—it makes them mature better. That's why I made sure that all of my kids worked when they were growing up.

Of course, life isn't all work. Not even for my mother!

Besides the animals and the vegetables, my mother also cared about beauty and she grew tons of flowers. She did a wonderful job with flowers and she won a number of awards for her gardens. As far as my mother is concerned, I guess the lesson is that if you want it all you have to have a goal and work toward it.

Then there's the curious story of the fig trees.

I'll get to Tunisia later on, but for now you should know that I would one day work in Tunisia in North Africa on a huge construction project.

So, just before I was to leave on one of my trips to Tunisia, my mother asked me to stop off in Italy and go to Gallinaro. Just a simple little side trip! She asked me to go to our land there, and she told me to go to one very specific fig tree and cut off two small sticks from a branch and to bring them home to her.

Because I was a dutiful son, that's exactly what I did. I went to our home in Gallinaro and found the exact tree and cut off two sticks—maybe twelve inches long. I put them in my briefcase and then flew home to America.

I got really nervous going through U.S. Customs—fearful that they would find the twigs and confiscate them, because you're not supposed to bring plant material into the country.

But they never asked me to open my briefcase. I made it through and got home and gave the sticks to my mother.

She nursed the two twigs and they grew! They were dormant and she nursed them back to life.

We had two fig trees!

But we were in Newton, Massachusetts, which gets a lot colder than Gallinaro, Italy. My father had to bury the little trees under the ground so that they would survive winter.

As the years went on and the trees got bigger, my mother built a tent-like structure and she snuck in a heater to keep the trees warm.

Eventually, she built a greenhouse around the trees.

And today, my sister and my brothers and I all have fig trees from those cuttings from Gallinaro.

They are very tasty figs. Really wonderful figs.

But, of course, more importantly, they are a taste from home—that my mother gave us.

A taste from Gallinaro.

Life was good in America.

I did well in school and upon my graduation from trade school, I decided to join the Marines because I felt it was my duty to give this beautiful new country my loyalty; even though I was of true Italian descent, I was making this pledge to America.

My big problem was that I didn't tell anyone, including my parents!

I didn't tell them that I had enlisted in the Marines. And I didn't tell them that I was about to leave for Paris Island, South Carolina, for my basic training in the morning.

The night before I was to leave—I can say that that was the longest night of my life.

BUILDING MY LIFE

CHAPTER THREE
Semper Fi

Why? Why the Marines? Why now?

That's what they asked me the next morning when I had to tell them I was leaving.

My mother was very upset. She refused to say goodbye to me. But she didn't have time to do anything about it. We all cried a little—but we hugged as well. Then it was time to leave.

Off I went to Paris Island in South Carolina for basic training.

Basic training was really tough. I did okay, but there were guys who had a rough time. I'd hear them crying at night. One guy smashed his trigger finger in a door jamb on purpose to get out of the service.

Thank God I came from a disciplined family. I was used to hard work and following orders and doing things when I was supposed to do things. So I made out all right.

And it wasn't long before my mother forgave me—of course she would—and started sending me care packages. Boxes of food! It was almost like being home.

I survived basic training and then got to go home for ten days. My parents were glad to see me.

I had made lots of new friends at boot camp, but, unfortunately, after boot camp we were dispersed to different areas.

I was off to active duty. All the way to Midway in the Pacific. After about eight months, they transferred me to Hawaii—to Marine Air Station Ewa on Oahu, about twenty miles west of Pearl Harbor. Ewa was hit during the attack on Pearl Harbor, and all forty-eight planes stationed there were destroyed. It was quickly rebuilt, of course, and became a major staging area during the war for Marines leaving for action in the Pacific. The Marines closed the base in 1952, because the runways were too short for jets.

I loved my stay at Ewa. I was assigned to the MPs, the Military Police. We had a lot of fun—a lot of adventures. But there was also a lot of discipline, a lot of marching. And we had to be sharp all the time.

I had a good relationship with everyone, especially with the cooks! I'd visit the kitchens a lot and became friends with them. I ate very well. The MPs had a special dining area and the cooks would bring my buddies and me extra food and special food. That was great—and it made me popular with my buddies.

Back then, the armed services were still segregated and the cooks and kitchen staff in the Marines and the Navy were African Americans. I became very friendly with them. Hey, we're all in this together, aren't we? We're all doing our best to serve our country.

Then it was Christmas. My first Christmas ever being away from home. As part of our MP duties, we'd frisk servicemen returning to the base from leaves and, usually, we'd confiscate a lot of liquor that they were trying to bring back to the base.

We'd turn over all liquor to the duty officer and it would end up in the Officers Club.

Well, it was Christmas Eve.

Because we were homesick, my buddy and I decided to keep a couple of bottles for ourselves. After we were off duty and had changed from our uniforms into regular clothes, we went outside next to our barracks and reminisced about our families and the Christmas celebrations that we would normally have.

After that, the only thing I remember was that I found myself sleeping on my bunk the next morning; I was told that I had been carried to my bunk by other friends.

I made a vow that I would never again lose control of my body. I've never been drunk since.

My tour on Ewa lasted eighteen months. I never went home during that time. I did my job as well as I could and I enjoyed it. And I saw a lot. For example, on Sundays I had to escort prisoners to and from church. I was Catholic and this was the first time I got to see other religions first hand. I enjoyed that. I've always enjoyed learning and exploration.

One of my buddies on Ewa was a pilot. After a while we became good friends, and he'd take me up! I got "flying lessons." Which meant I sat in the back seat of a fighter and hung on for dear life! But after a few flights he instructed me how to operate a fighter, which I truly enjoyed. Then one day he took me up and didn't tell me that he was practicing to "fly blind"—to fly with instruments only! The windshield was blackened. That was a little bit of education I could have done without.

I worked hard and never once got in trouble. I saw a lot of Hawaii. I went, naturally, to Pearl Harbor and saw the air base and the *Arizona* memorial and the service military cemetery. I'll never forget that.

I had lived so far in three very different worlds: Gallinaro, Massachusetts and Hawaii. What helped me was that I always saw my situation as having a job to do and I had to do it as best I could.

After twenty-four months, I was done.

Before my discharge, I was called before my commanding officer and he asked me why I didn't want to sign up for another hitch.

I told him that I had served my country and I was proud of that.

But now it was time for me to go home.

Now it was time to go home to my family.

CHAPTER FOUR
A Real Lunch

My mother was so glad to see me!

I had flown from Hawaii to San Diego and then to Chicago. It was January and it was windy and cold. I had forgotten how cold it could get! From Chicago, I took the train to Boston.

My brother Jerry met me in Boston and drove me home, to my family, to my mother and father and my sister and brothers.

My mother said that I was her favorite son and that she was glad to have me home—which made me feel bad in front of my siblings. Anyway, she forgave me for enlisting and we got along very well and everyone was happy.

I rested and enjoyed my mother's cooking.

Let me talk about her cooking.

I'm going to go back a bit and tell a story about food that you may not believe. But it's true. All of it. It happened my first year in America when I was twelve years old.

During that first summer vacation from school, I worked on a vegetable farm—the owner was Peter Volante and his farm was in Newton Centre. It was about fifty acres and it was all irrigated, which was amazing for the times. My hourly rate was seven-and-a-half cents an hour, which was pretty good. I worked each day from 7:00 A.M. to 6:00 P.M. We had an hour for lunch, which was necessary, because my mother packed me eighteen to twenty-one sandwiches a day—using Italian bread. You read that right. I would eat that many sandwiches each and every day. Some days she'd make individual sandwiches; some days she would take one whole loaf of good Italian bread, eighteen inches in diameter, and make one big sandwich. It would take me about forty-five minutes to consume my lunch.

I was a growing kid, I guess. I never got heavy. I've never been heavy.

And at dinner, after work, I'd have bowls and bowls of spaghetti or anything else that my mother had cooked. I don't believe that I ever weighed more than 140 pounds. My lunch bag was so large that my friends would ask me what I had in that bag, and I was too embarrassed to tell them it was my lunch, so I lied and told them it was my changing clothes, which they didn't believe.

Mangia, mangia.

After working a six-day week, I'd make six to seven dollars. I was so glad to give my pay to my dad; it made me feel that I was making my contribution.

I got an allowance of twenty-five cents a week. And every week, I spent it the same way. I'd go to the movies for ten cents. I'd spend five cents on popcorn or candy.

Then, with the remaining ten cents, I'd buy a blueberry pie one day a week for dessert after lunch, while working at the farm. Dessert! After twenty homemade sandwiches!

One doesn't understand the meaning of having blueberry pie, especially when you knew that you had to wait until the next week to be able to again buy something that you really enjoyed. I came to understand the value of money and to learn to do without until you had the funds to buy the things that you enjoyed.

I never forgot that during the many times when I was tired and hungry. I looked up in the sky and I prayed to God to be sure nothing would happen to my father so that we would not *starve*. God answered my prayers, and my father lived to be 93 years old.

Maybe that's part of the reason I always tried to be the best at whatever I did. If we were picking vegetables, I was a leader. If we were pulling weeds from celery rows, I led the pack. I always wanted to finish first. My boss promoted me the following year by giving me a raise to ten cents an hour and he also made me the leader of all the field workers. Finally, I was moved inside and worked in the washing room, getting produce ready for taking to the markets.

About four years later, I told my immediate boss that two other workers were starting their own farm and I was asked to go with them. When old man Peter Volante heard this, he went to see my father and pleaded with him to convince me to stay with them and not go with the new owners.

But my father said, "Whatever Pasquale wants—is his decision."

It really made me feel good that my dad trusted my decision.

So I went to work on the new farm with the new owners, and I stayed there until I graduated from trade school.

Then the Marines. Then home. Then more good food.

And now I was to embark on a whole new life.

But it was a life that never would have lunches like that again.

CHAPTER FIVE
On Our Own

Over the years, of course, my siblings and I went off on our own into the great big world.

My siblings are still living, except for my my oldest brother, Gerardo—Jerry—who passed away a number of years ago. Jerry and I were always very close—going all the way back to Gallinaro. I already wrote that whenever we had to walk somewhere, Jerry would carry me on his shoulders.

We'd look out for each other.

One day, back in Gallinaro, my brother got into huge trouble with my mother. Jerry loved hunting. He had a rifle of his own, but he always needed to buy more ammunition. One day, he needed money for gun powder and he took a few wheat sacks out of the wooden vault and carried them to town and sold them without telling my mother.

When my mother found out what had happened she was very upset. She gave Jerry a beating. He threatened to leave, so my mother got panicky and tied Jerry to the legs of his bed. I snuck into the room and brought him a blanket and food.

This went on for a couple of weeks. During the day, Jerry would work with my mother—tied with a rope around his legs to my mother's waist.

Jerry came to America with my father before the rest of us came. He and my father established themselves here, and then my father was able to bring the rest of us over.

Right after that, World War II erupted and Jerry joined the Construction Battalion, known, of course, as the Seabees. Part of the Navy, the Seabees worked courageously, under great danger, in the Pacific theater of war. They built roads and airstrips. They were often under fire as they worked. Jerry did well. He saw combat up close and did his duty.

After the war he was discharged and came home.

But then he went to Italy and married the girl I was supposed to marry!

Well, sort of. Her name is Carmella and she lived near us in Gallinaro, and I guess my mother and Carmella's mother thought they could arrange a marriage between Carmella and myself some day. But then we moved to America and that idea went away.

Anyway, Jerry married Carmella and took her back to our house in Newton to live. That didn't go well at all, because my mother was very hard on her new daughter-in-law. So I talked with my brother a lot and I convinced him that he and Carmella should move out of the house and get their own place.

They did, and everything worked out well. Carmella is a wonderful person and they had a very happy marriage.

Jerry went into house building. He had such a big heart that the homeowners would take advantage of him, and he didn't make as much money as he should have made. I helped him out a few times, and, finally, he came to work with me.

My big brother was a very gentle, very nice man. He was a good family person.

Next in line after Jerry was my brother Dominic, the second born.

He and I went into business together. He bought a dump truck with savings—and we were off and running. We started by doing odds and ends with builders—such as concrete work and landscaping and so on.

It went pretty well for a while. But one summer morning he took me to a new house that was being constructed and he said that I needed to dig a trench from the street to the house for the water line. It was about sixty feet long and five feet deep. It was a really hot summer day. I had no equipment. I had to do it by using a pick and a shovel. I had done a good job. It was nearly done, but it wasn't 100 percent done when Dominic showed up at 6:00 P.M. When he saw that it wasn't completely finished, he started yelling at me.

I tried to explain to him that I had worked really hard and it was much too much to expect one person to perform all this work in one day. He would not accept my explanation. So at that time I said to myself that this was not going to work; but I stayed with Dominic until the end of the year. At that point I was happy to get the accounting of the nice profit that we had made that year. But he gave me very little money with very little explanation. So at that point I told him that I couldn't continue to work with him and it would be best that we parted.

There wasn't any bad blood. We were too close for that. We were brothers. But I told him that I couldn't work for him anymore. He was okay. He understood.

We certainly remained close. He and his wife Alga have a great family, we all see each other from time to time.

I was the next born, but we'll skip me for the time being and move on to my sister Maria. She was the fourth child and the only girl.

In America, my mother was very tough on Maria. Maria could hardly ever go out; she couldn't wear makeup. My mother kept close tabs on her.

Maria went to high school and then she went to work in the Ucinite factory with my mother. I felt that Maria was held almost like in a prison by my mother, and I needed to get Maria away from my mother so she could start to live a normal life. So I offered her a job—to help her get out of the factory and be on her own. She came to work for me as a manager of a restaurant called the Bull in the Somerset Hotel in Boston. It was a steak house; lots of Red Sox and Bruins players came there for dinner and afterward they'd hang out at the nightclub called Flicks.

Eventually, I had to get Maria to be on her own so she could live life on her own. I decided to put her as a manager of my apartment complex in Nahant, Massachusetts, with the understanding that she would have to live in the complex.

My mother was very upset at all this and she didn't talk to either one of us for six months.

But it was good for Maria—to be on her own and have her own career—and, eventually, as always, my mother came around.

I guess it was hard for my mother too. All those years in Italy—with my father away—she had to do it all. That's a lot of pressure; that's a lot of responsibility. I think my mother could only survive and make things work by always being in tight control.

Anyway, we now get to Tony—the baby of the family.

I always respected Tony as my little brother—but that didn't stop me from kidding him all the time! I teased him about everything. I even would tell him that he was the older brother and that he had to take care of me.

He was always anxious to beat me at sports. But he never could. He still can't! Sometimes he would purposefully forget to record the correct score and he always favored toward himself. But he doesn't get away with it. I remember one time we were playing golf and he hit his ball in the woods. We went to help him find the ball and after spending much time with no luck, we saw a ball falling down his leg. I said that he couldn't do that and it cost him a penalty. He was not happy but he took it like a man. Then, again, he failed to remember the proper score, but I kept him honest. The same goes with skiing; when we would go skiing he was relegated to ski with me because I skied very hard and fast. He would like to take it easy. So I pushed him to be a better skier.

One time, we decided to go west to ski at Lake Tahoe. It was my daughter Patty, my brother Tony, his lovely wife Connie and me. We skied pretty hard each day. Then one night at dinner, Connie suggested that she and Patty would like to go shopping the next day—which meant that Tony had to ski with me. He admitted later that he didn't sleep well that night. The new day was beautiful. The sun was shining and I couldn't wait to get to the mountain. Once there, we made a couple of runs. Then the lines for the chair lift were getting long, so I suggested that we go to the singles line because hardly anybody was in it. That would allow us to make more runs.

However, at about 11:00 A.M., Tony told me he had to go to the restroom, and I said, "Okay but be sure to hurry back soon." In the meantime, I continued to ski. An hour and a half later, there was still no sign of Tony.

I took my skis off and went into the lodge looking for him. No sign of him in the dining room, so I went into the men's restroom; I checked all the stalls and I recognized his boots! He was sitting in the stall just resting—or hiding from me. I knocked on the door and he opened it; he was surprised that I had found him. I said, "Brother, you're not going to hide from me! Back to the mountain!"

We ended up having a great day. He slept really well that night.

The next day we returned to ski on the bigger mountain. After a couple of runs, Tony and Connie decided to ski on a beginner slope. After lunch, Tony joined Patty and me, while Connie went off to take a lesson and ski on the smaller trails. At the end of the day, Tony couldn't find Connie and he got very concerned. He reported to the ski patrol that he couldn't find his wife, and the ski patrol went ahead and dispatched its entire team to search for Connie.

After a couple of hours of searching with no luck, my daughter Patty finally found Connie reading a book by the fireplace! Connie was totally unaware of the confusion she had caused.

And then, to add one more little element, Tony couldn't find his street shoes. What a day!

Even today, after all these years, I remember all that very clearly. I don't remember Tony ever skiing with me again. But he is always so much fun to be with.

After Tony finished high school, he went into the Air Force and when he returned he also went into building houses. He and Dominic decided to go into the general-construction business and they came to me for advice and direction, which I was happy to give. In fact, I gave them one of my best estimators and I also gave them office space in my building so that we could be near each other if they needed more help.

Tony married a great girl—Connie. She's a very strong-willed lady and a great athlete. She, too, always beats Tony in tennis, but it doesn't bother him.

Tony and I have always been very close—we joke and kid a lot.

Our whole family is close. We enjoy each other's company—as do all of our children.

Okay, now let's get back to me and how I went off on my own.

When I was in the Marines, I had been paid $52 a month. I kept $10 and sent the rest home. Ten dollars was enough for me. And I was happy to help out at home. When I was discharged, my mustering-out pay came to a little bit over $300.

Once I got home, I was expected to turn over my job earnings to my father to help the family. But, there was an exception to this rule—age. I was now over 21 years old and therefore I was obligated to only pay for room and board, which I did for as long as I lived at home with my parents.

I took my $300 from the Marines and I spent $150 on a car. You always remember your first car—mine was an old Pontiac.

That left me a blance of $150—which I used as the capital to start my business. I used part of it to buy needed tools: a wheelbarrow, shovels, a pick and masonry tools. When I say "I," that's what I mean. It was just me. I was officially on my own. All alone, on my own. And I had to get work!

I approached a builder who was constructiong a house on Chestnut Street in West Newton and gave him a price for a concrete floor, a chimney and all of the landscaping. He looked me over very carefully and, finally, he gave me the job!

It would have been good—if I had known how to build a chimney.

You must understand that I had never done any cement finish work or laid any bricks in my whole life, but I had confidence and guts that I could do it. So, here I was, all by myself, and I started to build the chimney. I mixed my own mortar and stacked the bricks on a work station and I started laying bricks!

Unfortunately, the chimney didn't go up straight. I took it down three times before I was satisfied with the workmanship.

I now needed to do the cellar floor. So I asked a buddy of mine to help, but he also had no experience in cement finish work. We set to it and we put in the cement floor, the front walk and the steps. Finally, I did all the landscaping.

For the fireplace in the living room, I brought in my father to show me how to do it.

So, this first job was done—and done to my satisfaction. The builder was happy to see the work completed. And most of all, I got paid!

I got other jobs. Then I hired my first employee. Rico Bianchi. The same Rico Bianchi who was my friend and translator in grammar school.

At this point, I approached other builders, from whom I was looking to get similar contracting work: landscaping, masonry work and concrete work. Besides Rico, my laborer, I also hired an older mason—Mr. Crosetti. He was a gem of a person and he really took a liking to me. In fact, if he knew I was tight for money, he'd delay cashing his weekly check to help me out. Eventually, he'd ask me if it was all right to cash a few checks. I told him to go ahead. Mr. Crosetti stayed with me until he got sick and finally passed away. I will never forget that man; he was like a father to me.

Unfortunately, it's more and more difficult to find that type of person today. I've always tried as hard as possible to be loyal to bosses and workers—and to help people out if I could. I don't see that today like I used to. If you spend your entire life worrying only about yourself, you'll miss most of the things worth having and doing.

Anyway, with Mr. Crosetti's help, I landed more and more jobs. Eventually, I became the largest masonry contractor in the Boston area. My company was Pat Franchi Mason Contractor Company.

That really felt good. I knew I was accomplishing something and I was proud of our work and the progress I was making.

It came to a point that I wanted to expand, so that I could do larger masonry jobs, besides doing masonry for house builders.

Success requires knowledge. And hard work. And perseverance.

The first thing I realized was that I had to go to night school, to learn how to read blueprints and learn how to create a proper estimate.

I did that, and then I got more help from experts.

I was friends with Larry Tocci who owned a large construction company, Tocci Bros. I would go to his office after work and he'd show me how to read blueprints.

He told me how to figure out how many bricks it would take to fill an area of one square yard. He did the same for figuring concrete work. This was so I could come up with accurate prices. This went on for several months until I felt sure I knew what I was doing.

Business was moving ahead, but I was not satisfied with doing only masonry work for house builders. I was thinking more and more of embarking on a new direction—I wanted to start doing masonry work for general contractors on large-scale jobs such as warehouses, schools, apartment complexes and so on. I did go in that direction and I was doing well.

Then I discovered a catch that was holding me back from expanding. Even though I was making a profit, I was held back because the general contractors would keep retainage from me until they would get it from the owners which would not take place until many months after I had completed my work. This was hurting my financial position since I had to meet the payroll and purchase all the material for the job—and, of course, I could not hold back a retainage from my suppliers or laborers.

I had to figure out how to resolve this matter—which I did and which you will read about a little later.

Right now, let me tell you that I was happy about how my business was going, but as for how my life was going—well, that depended on Madeline.

CHAPTER SIX
Madeline

I met Madeline Corsi when I was twelve years old and she was only nine.

Soon after we came to the United States, our family was invited to dinner at the Bernard Corsi house, since the Corsi family came from the same area in Italy as my parents did. Anyway, I saw this beautiful young lady by the name of Madeline. At that time, she was only nine years old and I was only twelve. I immediately fell in love with her, and I said to myself that one day I was going to marry her!

I know this will all sound a bit odd, but back then, even at age twelve, I had a vision. Or maybe I had a number of visions.

I wanted to go to school and do well and live and work in America and be successful. So I set out to learn what I had to learn and to work hard and spend money wisely.

And I knew—defintely knew—that when we were older I would someday marry this beautiful young girl. I never lost sight of that vision. And when the right time came, I proposed and she accepted.

That's what I've always done.

That's what I've told my children.

You have to have a vision to be happy—and you have to be determined and work hard to make it come true.

But going back to when Madeline and I first met, well I could not see her often because we were too young and lived quite far away from each other.

But my family and her family belonged to a social organization called the Saint Marco Society, which had a family gathering once a year, and I can't tell you how much I looked forward to those parties so that I could see Madeline again. Unfortunately, I had to wait a whole year between events!

Finally, six years later, I got enough courage to ask her if I could take her out on her fifteenth birthday. My heart was pounding so fast, I thought I would have a heart attack! She accepted and that made it all right. But, she accepted with the understanding that I also needed to get approval from her parents.

So I went to see her father and mother. Luckily, they said yes—with the stipulation that we would be home no later than 11:00 P.M.

I took her to the RKO in Boston to see Benny Goodman and his orchestra. Afterwards, we stopped for a pizza and I kept looking at my watch to be sure I'd be home on time. Which we were. It was a wonderful evening.

From then on, we spoke on the phone from time to time.

Then I joined the Marines.

We corresponded by mail. I was good at writing letters, and she and I wrote each other all the time when I was away. Maybe that was one reason I never got in any trouble with the local grass-skirt ladies when I was in Hawaii.

Once I got home, we started dating again, and the more I saw her, the more I wanted to be with her.

One night I took Madeline to the movies. I knew that the next morning I had to go to a job site very early to meet a bricklayer, so I had loaded the trunk of my car full of the bricks that I would need in the morning to build a fireplace. On the way home from the movies, after I dropped off Madeline, I got a flat. Which meant that I had to take all of the bricks out of the trunk to get the jack and the spare tire out! I got the tire fixed. I got the bricks back in the trunk.

I said to myself, I have to marry this lady. I can't do this again.

In 1953, I found the courage to ask Madeline to marry me. She said yes! And I got the blessing of both sets of parents and a date was set.

However, during this time, my mother and Madeline's parents had some sort of argument about the wedding. I was still living at home and my mother said to me that the wedding was off! And she said that if I was going ahead with it, she was not coming to the wedding. I told her that the wedding was going to take place whether she approved or not.

So I packed up and left my parents' house.

"I'm marrying this girl whether you like it or not," I said to my mother on my way out of the house.

I moved into a boarding house. Except for the Marines, it was my first time on my own. The landlady liked me a lot. When I moved out, she gave me a two-dollar bill—and said, "Here, take this and you'll never be broke."

I still cry when I think of that.

Obviously, things would work out with the families and everyone came and had a grand time.

It was a wonderful wedding on February 2, 1951, at Our Lady's Church in Newton. After the reception, we drove off to Miami for our honeymoon.

We lived with Madeline's parents for a while. But then, as always happens, we decided to move out and set up our own house. I built the house myself. It was at 16 Mount Vernon Terrace in West Newton. We chose West Newton because Madeline's parents had moved to West Newton and she wanted to be close to her family.

When we moved in, we had a nice house, if I say so myself, but we had no furniture. All we had was a kitchen table with two chairs; two other chairs in the living room; and a bed and a bureau in the bedroom.

My mother came to visit and she saw what we had for furniture, so she bought us a dining room set and after that things slowly began to take shape.

Madeline and my mother became very close, which made my life much, much easier.

I enjoyed Madeline's company tremendously, and I'd try to come home for lunch if I was nearby. Maybe not twenty sandwiches, but still a hearty lunch.

One day after lunch, as I was leaving to go back to work, Madeline asked what I'd like for dinner.

I thought a second and said, "Prosciutto bone and rice."

When I came home for dinner, I found Madeline crying.

"What's wrong?" I asked.

"Look," she said. "Look at the kitchen."

She had boiled a pound of rice in a small pan and then in a second pan and then a third pan. The rice exploded! Like in a movie. There was rice everywhere.

I started laughing and we cleaned it all up and there was still a lot left in the pots for dinner!

That little episode aside, Madeline was a wonderful cook.

And, although we struggled to make ends meet, we enjoyed our life a great deal.

One day, I noticed that Madeline always wore the same dress every time we would go to visit someone or go out to dinner with our friends.

I said, "Why don't you go buy another dress?"

"But we have to make ends meet," she said.

This went on for a long time, so I decided to take the matter into my own hands; one night, when she was in bed, I got the dress and ripped it to shreds. In the morning, I showed it to her and said, "Now you have to buy another dress."

So she did.

We always laughed about that.

During this time—even though we were busy raising a family, and with me trying very hard to build a business—we managed to find time to socialize with our friends. We took some vacations by ourselves, just to be alone together.

Madeline was not very athletic, but she tried very hard just to keep me happy. So one night during dinner, I suggested that we should take dancing lessons and she jumped at this idea! We signed up for a bunch of lessons at the Arthur Murray Studio and, believe it or not, we both really enjoyed dancing and we looked pretty good doing it.

However, at this time in my life, I had a very bad habit.

Chain smoking.

I started smoking in the Marines—to help me stay awake at night when I was on guard duty outdoors in the boondocks, and also when I was doing the graveyward shift at the main post gate. When you're on guard from midnight to 8:00 A.M., it can get quite lonely around 3:00 A.M., and it helped to smoke a cigarette.

And I just kept smoking afterwards.

I would get up in the morning and I would light up a cigarette even before my breakfast. I would put out a cigarette just before going to sleep. I was averaging four packs of cigarettes a day. I knew this habit was bad and I tried very hard to stop. I tried to smoke cigars or a pipe, but no dice.

Finally, at one event, Madeline and I were really cutting the rug. But during a very fast polka, I almost passed out! I knew it was because I was smoking too much. On the way home, I told Madeline that I was stopping smoking, and of course she laughed.

But I said, "This time it's for real."

I asked her to please give me space and be patient with me and ask the children to do the same.

So what did I do?

I took three packages of cigarettes. I put one in my night table next to my bed. The second went into the glove compartment in my car. And the third went on top of my desk. I did that so that each time I got a desire to smoke, I'd take a cigarette out of the package and I'd speak to it. I would say that I was stronger than it was—and I crushed it into bits in my fist.

This went on for a couple of months, but I finally conquered this bad habit. I now look back and I say to myself how did my poor wife stand that terrible cigarette odor?

And I felt great. I never felt better. I still feel great.

While all this was going on, with our marriage and our home and my business, I had my office in our house. It was convenient and didn't take up too much space.

Then we had our first child—Linda. And after that, we had Debra. And then came Patricia and Susanne. We kept trying for a boy, and we soon had Louie and Michael.

But after our second child, Debra, was born, Madeline said it was time for me to move out of the house and into an office. So I did. I rented a small office in Newtonville, not far from my house. At the time I was doing al lot of masonry work for a builder named Mr. Goldman—and he needed an office and asked me if he could share part of my office. I said okay and we got along really well. But then I began to expand quite a bit, and one day I had to say to Mr. Goldman that the office was too small for both of us and one of us must leave.

He looked at me and said, "I really think it's best for you to go, since you are very passionate about your work and you will need a lot more space."

So I did. I built my own office on Webster Street in West Newton. A few years later I overgrew this space and I moved to 425 Watertown Street in Newton.

It was good to need more space—it meant things were going well. I was doing more and more masonry work and I needed to hire more people—and I needed more office space for files and storage and meetings and so on.

I missed being home with Madeline, but, as always, she was right. Work should be separate from home. It turned out great and we were very happy.

CHAPTER SEVEN
I Had a Vision

Business was good, but, because I worked for general contractors and builders, I often found myself begging them for my money. It was very aggravating and I was sick and tired of it. So I decided to become my own general contractor—because, as a general contractor, I would get paid by the owners first and then I would turn around and pay my suppliers and subcontractors.

By the way, as I've said, my brothers Dominic, Jerry and Tony also flourished, building lots of houses for returning GIs and their families. I also tried to build homes, but I found out that it wasn't for me. So I started doing masonry work and small jobs.

I also started putting in bids on government buildings around Air Force bases. These bids included dining halls, barracks, hospitals and missile sites—along with many alterations to existing buildings.

Yet again, my thinking was that if you have a vision and you follow it—you do what you have to do—then it will usually work out. That's what happened with military work. I started getting jobs; and those jobs led to other jobs. We did good work—excellent work. We did the jobs on time and on budget.

After a while, I had a very good reputation and my company was given a special classification for completing work on time, with good workmanship.

We worked on many buildings at Limestone Air Force Base in Limestone, Maine. Today, it is known as Loring Air Force base, but back then it was the largest base in the Air Force's Strategic Air Command.

We also did a lot of work at Dow Air Force Base, in Bangor, Maine. Originally, it had been a private, commercial air field. During World War II it was turned into Dow Air Force base, and, today, it is the Bangor Air National Guard Base. When we worked there, we built the dining hall, the hospital, barracks and homes for the officers' families.

At Otis Air Force Base, in Buzzards Bay on Cape Cod, Massachusetts, we built the first defensive missile site in the country. We also built the dining hall, a barracks and a small hospital.

We then did a lot of work at Chicopee Air Force Base, which is near Springfield, Massachusetts. It was the largest air force base in the country, in terms of area; and until recently it served as a backup landing site for the space shuttle.

Then we worked at Fort Devens, in Ayer, Massachusetts, which is an Army Reserve Base. We built barracks, the hospital, the Officers Club and many other smaller buildings and officers' housing.

In the meantime, we were also busy with non-military projects throughout New England.

In Burlington, Vermont, we did a lot of work, such as putting up the new Federal Building and remodeling part of the Mary Fletcher Hospital. At the University of Vermont, we built dormitories, classrooms and a field house.

We did work for the telephone company, putting up many buildings in the New England area. These are the classic brick buildings that are identified simply by how they look.

One of my most interesting jobs was the construction of buildings designed by the American architect Paul Rudolf for the Southeastern Massachusetts Technological Institute in North Dartmouth. Rudolf was the Dean of the Yale School of Architecture, and he was known for his daring and innovative use of concrete. For example, the university library looks like a wild sailing ship, with concrete and glass elements coming out of the edifice at all angles and directions. It is concrete in motion. I took my daughter Linda to the opening ceremonies and I asked her what she thought of the design and she replied that she thought it reminded her of an octopus.

Things moved ahead. It was post-World War II—the boom of the 1950s—and I was in the right place at the right time. Luck and timing are important—but nothing happens without vision. I knew that I needed to be bigger. And I knew that the boom we were living in would be the right time to make it all happen. It did. Eventually, I had 650 employees!

But let me back up a bit.

As I've written, when my lovely wife kicked me out of the house, I rented a small office in Newtonville and shared it with Mr. Goldman, a builder with whom I had done lots of work. We shared space and a receptionist. Like I've said, you have to have a base of operations, but you don't need frills. I kept on growing and hired estimators, and then I had overgrown the office and I decided to build a new office on Webster Street in West Newton.

At this time I decided it was time for me to incorporate. I chose to name my firm Franchi Construction Company, Inc. Of course, I needed an attorney to incorporate my new business, and ever since that date I have been paying legal bills. But the simple fact of life is that you can't live without lawyers.

One reason I believe I was able to be successful was that I was able to perform most of the work myself, which gave me control over speed and workmanship. Most other general contractors would subcontract out their work, which made them lose control and cut into the bottom line. I promise I won't say this again—well, maybe I will—but I had the vision to maximize profits by eliminating middle men. I knew it had to work. It only made sense that it would work. And once I got it up and running, sure enough, it did work.

We continued to build hospitals, schools, universities and apartment buildings—mostly in New England.

But, you know, you do a good job and people talk good about you.

I was asked by my bonding company if I was interested in completing a very sizable apartment complex in St. Louis, Missouri. The project had gone bust.

I said yes, and we took over the job. I went in, figured out what went wrong and what had to be done. Four years later, I finished it. The developers were very pleased with the outcome.

A little closer to home, I also did a lot of work at UMass Amherst.

And then—a really interesting project came along. The Army Corps of Engineers hired us to build an underground command headquarters for controlling the deployment of our weapons systems in the Northeast. It was to be on the *inside* of Mt. Tom in South Hadley, Massachusetts.

We had to hollow out part of the interior of the mountain!

It had to be able to withstand a nuclear attack.

We used huge digging machines to hollow out the interior of the mountain, and then on the inside we had to line the entire structure with reinforced concrete. Even the doors had to be able to survive an atomic blast; we built huge structures made of reinforced steel and concrete. It was a great success—made even more so because it was the only time the Army Corps of Engineers negotiated a contract with the Franchi Construction Company, rather than putting it out to bid, which they would normally do because of high-security requirements. They had confidence in us and we didn't let them down.

We finished the job and, thankfully, it was never tested, but I know it could certainly withstand a nuclear attack.

We really had a lot of jobs. We had work going on in many different areas and we were putting up many different types of buildings.

I had at least eight-to-ten jobs going at the same time. I was building apartment complexes, schools and hospitals all over New England.

Still, this wasn't enough for me. I had to go further.

All the way to the moon.

Well, sort of.

I'll get to this in a later chapter, but for now let me say that I would someday get a huge contract for Cape Canaveral—Cape Kennedy—building a lot of the infrastructure for NASA. One of the most exciting projects was the main launch pad for the Mercury program.

But first, I want to talk about land.

CHAPTER EIGHT
Land

I had another vision. There. I said it again. But it's the simple truth. While the construction company was going full blast, I decided it was a good time to get into real estate.

It was a profitable venture. But what I really liked was the idea of bringing old buildings back to life again.

My first project was to buy a building near Government Center and Faneuil Hall in Boston, across the street from Boston City Hall and next door to the famous Oyster Bar. We rehabbed it into office and retail space.

The ground floor was rented to a young lady by the name of Betty. She was well known in town and she built a very elegant bar and restaurant. I liked the way she renovated the restaurant and bar. Lots of dark wood. Classic look.

Very, very classic—like Betty herself, who named the bar Betty Rolls Royce. Betty was flamboyant. She drove a yellow Rolls Royce and always parked it right outside the bar. It was a drawing card. Sort of a movable billboard. She was in her mid-forties, but she always surrounded herself with very young people. She was a magnet for the young and the restless and the party goers.

Oh—this is funny—every day she would get a ticket for illegally parking her car.

She didn't care. She thought of it as renting advertising space!

Building on that success, I bought two more buildings.

The Hotel Vendome on Commonwealth Avenue and Dartmouth Street; and the Somerset Hotel, also on Commonwealth Avenue.

The Somerset project went very smoothly—and we eventually converted it to apartment and office space. It was—and is—a very luxurious place to live. And as I've written, it had a very successful restaurant called the Bull, which specialized in prime beef. It also had a nightclub called Flicks, which was very exclusive—all the Red Sox and Bruins players would hang out there. There were long lines to get in. Flicks was well done. It was a place where you went to be seen. I brought in entertainers from Las Vegas to perform at Flicks. To show how popular the place was, there came a time when I had to change my home phone to an unlisted number because friends would be calling me very late at night to ask if I could get them into the club.

The Vendome Hotel was another matter entirely—a tragic story that I still think about all the time.

Built in 1871, and expanded in 1881, the Vendome was a luxury hotel, the premier hotel in Boston. It was built in the classic French style—with a Mansard roof and what they call Second Empire details. Everything about it was top of the line. The rich and the famous stayed there.

But when I came into the picture, the building had been abandoned for a long time—it was deteriorating. There had been four small fires and the roof was partially open to the weather. It was in very bad shape when I bought it. But—the "bones" were good. It had a lot of architectural taste. And the furnishings—the furniture and the mirrors and tables—were antiques. It had once been spectacular. But now it was time to clean house.

It was all boarded up and there was three feet of water in the basement. I saw through all that. I saw the potential of what this building could look like again. Not to mention that it had a great location.

I was also the first developer in this area to build condominiums. It was a very new idea that the state had just approved.

So I went and hired a good architect and got to work. Everything went smoothly. We got within two weeks of finishing the first units. We were ready to advertise the open house and the sale of two-bedroom condos for $25,000 to $35,000—which in 1972 wasn't cheap, but was well worth it. Today, some units are selling for over $500,000.

One day—June 17, 1972—was a day that started out like any other day. I took my son Louie to Pop Warner practice. Then I went home and started packing because I had to go to Tunisia to visit a huge construction project we were involved with—but that story comes later.

Madeline asked if I was hungry, and I said I was. I asked her to make me a sandwich. While I was eating, I turned on the TV and I started watching the Red Sox. We were playing the White Sox. Bill Lee was pitching for us and Eddie Kasko was our manager. Suddenly the TV announcer—Ken Coleman—said that he could see a lot of smoke in the distance—and he said that he thought it was near Commonwealth Avenue. I didn't think much about it and continued to have my sandwich until Ken Coleman came back and said that he thought that the Vendome Hotel was on fire. I almost choked on my sandwich and rushed to tell Madeline what I had heard.

I dropped my unfinished sandwich and I drove into Boston. Sure enough—to my horror—it was the Vendome Hotel that was on fire. A raging fire.

There were trucks and men and hoses and water and chaos everywhere.

I found the fire chief and I told him that I was the developer and that I knew all about the building—inside and out—and I'd help in any way I could.

He looked at me and said, "You take care of construction—I'll take care of the fire."

And he walked away.

I could only watch.

A while later, my construction superintendent and my staff attorney arrived. They too had heard of the fire and came to see what was happening.

We watched in horror as the fire got worse.

One section of the building had a flat roof. There was a parapet wall, about four feet high, that ran all around the perimeter of the roof. It had a great view of the city—in fact, they used to have dances on that roof at night, back when the original hotel was a hot spot and an elegant place to go to be seen.

Flames were shooting out of the roof and from the windows below, and some of the firemen were inside of the building while others were continuing to pump water. I knew how bad this looked and I feared the worst.

I said to my superintendent, "If they continue pumping that large amount of water in that area, that roof is going to collapse."

It was terrible. It was terrible that it happened. It was terrible that no one listened. It was terrible that we couldn't prevent it.

As everyone knows, the roof did collapse. It was because the area up there was like a huge bathtub full of water.

Nine firemen were killed.

It was a terrible, terrible day. The worst firefighting tragedy in Boston history.

I went to all the funerals. I was lost in grief.

There were many investigations, of course, and thank God that no fault was found from my company.

That was small solace compared to the lives lost.

Eventually, we got back to work and we finished the project. All the condo units were sold. Today, units sell for $500,000. It's a really beautiful building. I often wonder if the younger owners know of the awful price that was paid.

After that project was done, we moved on to other things.

I built a very elegant apartment complex called Cabot Estates in Jamaica Plain in Boston. This had been the land of the famous Cabot family. There was a beautiful family mansion that we renovated and divided into apartments, and then we built several large apartment buildings on the land adjacent to the mansion.

I could have lived in the mansion, of course, but I was happy where I was.

But my children moved into different apartments in the mansion when they got married.

Cabot Estates is across the street from the tall Jamaica Towers complex—that I also built.

I have really enjoyed these real estate ventures. Especially renovation projects—because, like I said, it's great to see something come alive again.

I could have taken over the Faneuil Hall renovation. In fact Boston Mayor Kevin White asked me to take over the whole project—but it was too big for me at the time, considering all the other things I was doing.

Besides, I was still hurting from what happened to the Vendome site.

At this time, I had the contract to build both the Mass Pike Towers and the Tai-Tung Apartments—two very nice apartment complexes in the city of Boston. These buildings are three-to-ten stories high, designed to be all precast-concrete structures. We were in the middle of erecting the fourth floor of the first building when one of the wall panels disengaged from our crane; it fell to the ground and it smashed in pieces.

Thank God it happened then! Because we investigated and found out that the supplier had failed to install the reinforcing steel in the panels, as was specified in the plans. We had to take down every panel we had erected and start over from scratch. Well, the supplier went bankrupt. But we pressed on and we finished the work and people moved in and no further problems have occurred.

Business never stopped.

After the Mass Pike Towers and the Tai-Tung Village, we we were involved in building and renovating the VA Hospital in Bedford, Massachusetts. The entire hospital. I was very proud of the result—especially the new chapel. It was beautiful and peaceful.

CHAPTER NINE
Bella Luna

What to do next?

What's the next vision—and where would it lead me?

Space.

It turned out to be space.

What happened was that I had become really close to a number of people in the Army Corps of Engineers. We talked a lot about the boom going on at Cape Canaveral. So I decided to look into it. I opened an office in Titusville, Florida, and sent down my chief estimator.

Once we got our first contract, I sent down one of my best project managers. And, of course, I would go down myself every other week or so.

We started getting some small buildings to construct, such as a central fire station, some supply and receiving buildings and the spacecraft test complex. In that latter building, they actually tested the engines before they attached them to the spacecraft.

As time went on, and as we did well, we got a lot more assignments.

The two most interesting projects we were to work on were the NASA headquarters building and Launch Complex #14.

The Kennedy Space Center Headquarters had to house everything involved with the operation of NASA. Three stories high, it included the offices for the director and management staff—and it had more than 400,000 square feet of space.

BUILDING MY LIFE

The most famous part of this structure was the "brain room"—the mission control room. This was the place that was to become so very familiar to TV viewers—with all those rows of men and women sitting at computer terminals, monitoring the pre-flight status and then the launch and the mission and then recovery. I'm sure everyone remembers some very tense moments—as well as some very joyful ones. And those people were always so calm! And profesional. They spoke in even voices. They never showed alarm. They never panicked. They were Americans. And they were going to the moon.

Perhaps the most intriguing space we built was the offices of Werner Von Braun. Known as the "Father of Rocket Science," Von Braun developed rockets in Germany during World War II. After the war, he and other scientists were secretly taken to the United States—and went to work on our rocket programs. His biggest triumph, of course, was to lead the team responsible for the giant Saturn V rocket that blasted the Apollo missions into space and, eventually, to the moon.

Without a doubt, the most nerve-wracking part of our job at the Cape was the work on Launch Complex #14.

This was the site used to send up four manned Mercury missions—including Friendship 7, which was John Glenn's historic flight on February 20, 1962, to become the first American to orbit the Earth. The complex was also used to send up seven unmanned Mercury capsules.

First, we rebuilt and enlarged the office space where all personnel worked who were involved with launch and recovery. That was relatively easy—being straightforward construction.

Then there was Launch Complex #14—which turned out to be an entirely different experience.

In addition to the huge pad that held the rocket, there was also the gigantic launch tower which had to be erected. The tower itself was designed by another company. It was to be 300-feet high—that's equal to the length of a football field. And the width was equal to one half the width of a football field.

The sections for the tower were built by a fabricator in Alabama, under the supervision of the Army Corp of Engineers. My responsibility, under our contract, was to assemble the sections once they arrived and to erect the tower on the launch pad.

A big problem occurred when we started to examine the welding on the joints on each cross section of the tower. The welds didn't look so good at all. We called this matter to the attention of the Army Corps of Engineers inspector. He asked us to take X-rays of the welds. We did and they showed that the welds were defective. This was a huge problem because we were working on a tight schedule, since NASA already had a date for the first launch.

To remove all the welds and re-do them would take forever. But that's what had to be done!

I was directed to remove all the defective welds and re-weld the joints to be sure they were done properly.

It could be done, but it had to be done quickly to meet the scheduled launch date. Furthermore, it was understood that all this work would be done initially at my expense. Then I would submit a claim afterwards.

This put a huge financial strain on my company.

I had no choice but to do it. We set up a plan to address how we could do all this work in a very short time. My supervisors and I came up with the idea of setting up gigantic temporary tents so that we could work seven days a week, twenty-four hours a day. We used three crews of welders, with each crew being responsible for one third of the tower. Then we had another crew examining the new welds to ensure they were done right. And if that wasn't enough pressure, we had several Army inspectors looking over our shoulders all the time. And *then*—we had a very ignorant Lt. Colonel as our contract officer. He insisted on having daily meetings with project managers and me, as well as with the owners of all of my subcontractor firms, to evaluate our progress on a daily basis.

The Lt. Colonel kept making demands and pounding on us. It took up a huge amount of our time; time that we couldn't afford to lose. Furthermore, he kept talking down to us like we were morons. We'd leave those meetings angry and stressed out.

I was so upset I could barely stand it any more.

In the meantime, my beautiful wife had given birth to our son Louie, and there I was, stuck in Florida, arguing with this Lt. Colonel each and every day!

Finally, one day, I had reached the point where I simply couldn't stand the guy another moment. We couldn't do anything more than what we were already doing.

I took his progress schedule from him and ripped it to pieces in front of everyone and said, "You're causing nothing but trouble!"

I really screamed at him, using some words I probably shouldn't have.

I laid into him. I told him we were losing time because of him. I told him to stop interfering with our crew. And a few more words I shouldn't have used.

But I did say that we were doing the very best that we could. And if he didn't think so then he should cancel my contract and call my bonding company. Then we all walked out of the meeting.

The Lt. Colonel never asked to meet with us again. The job was done on time, and the launch took place on time.

After the incident with the Lt. Colonel, I rushed home to the hospital. In those days, women usually stayed in the hospital for five or six days after giving birth. I was determined to get there before Madeline went home with Louie.

I learned that the nurses were taking bets as to whether or not I'd make it in time to check her out.

I made it.

Madeline wasn't happy that I was late, but she fully understood my trouble and we worked it out. A new baby has a way of making everything all right.

But then, when I returned to Cape Canaveral, I learned something about being a man, about being a parent—because a sad thing happened that really affected me.

I got a call one day at my Newton office from my main concrete supplier in Florida, Mr. Rinker. He asked me when I was coming down to Cape Canaveral again. I told him, and he said he'd meet me at the airport. I thought this was strange. I checked with my comptroller and confirmed that Mr. Rinker's bills were all paid. So why this urgent call?

Sure enough, he was there when I landed and we talked and he gave me some bad news.

He told me that two of my key top people—who had been working for me for ten years or more—had been contracting work outside of my company and charging the expense to my company and keeping the payments for themselves.

They were stealing from me, on a large scale.

This not only hurt me—both personally and financially—but it hurt my relationship with many of my suppliers.

I was so depressed. I was betrayed. I couldn't believe it.

I called the sheriff and reported it and the two men were arrested.

That night, at my hotel, I couldn't sleep. I cried. I had trusted them. I paid them well. We were good friends. Why? Why?

In the early morning, I realized that although they had hurt me, they had also hurt their families—their children and their wives.

Can you imagine reading in the newspaper that your father is a crook? So I went to the police station and told the sheriff that I had made a mistake. I dropped all charges and I had them released.

I let them go, but I told them I never wanted to see them again. And I haven't.

They were remorseful. They were also grateful that I spared them.

The Cape was a boom town then, with NASA building everything in sight and with lots and lots of money being spent. They got caught up in it and thought they'd get away with it because everyone was doing it.

They would have gotten away with it, if it hadn't been for my friend who called me.

That incident could not, of course, diminish our accomplishment at Cape Canaveral.

We worked at the Cape for ten or twelve years. It was exhilarating. And when the Mercury missions soared into space—well, I was a little proud of our contributions.

I brought my family down to the Cape a number of times. My father was very impressed. I was so glad he got to see it. We saw several launches.

True, we didn't go into space ourselves—but we gave those that did a bit of a push to get them on their way.

CHAPTER TEN
Over There

You might think that there couldn't be a vision to follow after going to space.

And yet, I found one.

Tunisia.

Why in the world would I go to North Africa?

The simple answer—as I'm sure you can guess—is that I had a new vision. I saw a new way to expand the company—to make it grow.

I heard about A.I.D.—Agency for International Development—a U.S. federal-aid program for foreign countries. I looked into it—I was never afraid to put myself out there—and I started bidding on international projects.

Before I knew it, I was in a plane on my way to Tunisia.

A.I.D. wanted to help Tunisia build the University of Tunis, and I was flying there to see what it was all about and to figure out how to bid on it. I went by myself to save money. Besides, I don't see how anyone could have helped me, because none of my employees spoke Arabic! The job was huge. The goal was to build administrative buildings for the university and also for its law school, as well as classroom buildings and dining halls.

My ambition was to go international. To do something more advantageous and interesting. And this fit the bill. I got to Tunisia and went to Tunis to look at the site. There was nothing there. Nothing at all. Just a lot of land. I had sets of plans. It helped a bit that I knew the architectural firm, because they had a small office in Rome and I had worked with them before.

I started meeting with subcontractors. They spoke Arabic and French. I knew next to no French and no Arabic at all. I used my hands a lot and pointed at drawings and muddled along.

After five days of this, almost like throwing darts at a target, I put in a bid. It was the low bid! I won the contract. Was this a good thing or a bad thing? Time would tell.

We had to build administrative buildings, a classroom building and an auditorium. Other countries were participating as well—including Russia and France. We had our own piece of the pie.

A.I.D. had strict rules. There was all kinds of paperwork and regulations. The biggest thing was that, except for cement and gravel, everything—everything—had to be shipped over from the United States! I guess the idea was to help Tunisia—but not to hurt American business.

Since the buildings were designed to be made with exposed architectural concrete, we had to ship plywood from the United States— because plywood is what concrete forms are made with when you construct with exposed architectural concrete. We also needed form ties and plumbing fixtures and heating and air-conditioning fixtures. And doors and windows. On and on it went.

I had to send my key employees to Tunis; these included the project manager, superintendents, carpenters and cement finishers—along with all their tools! The government of Tunisia prohibited any kind of power equipment to be used at the job site. For example, all the excavation was by pick and shovel.

We hired locals to do construction work. But, like I said, we couldn't use heavy equipment. No cranes. No bulldozers. We hired more than 200 workers and they used picks and shovels and donkeys.

Yes, donkeys.

In an age of giant earth diggers, we used a row of donkeys to move dirt. Each donkey had a barrel on both sides. They were trained to walk slowly past a line of men with shovels. The men would shovel dirt into the barrels. When the donkeys got to the spot where the dirt was to be dropped, they would stop and a worker would open the bottoms of the barrels and the dirt fell out! Then the donkeys went back to where the men were digging and started all over again. This went on from sunrise to sunset—seven days a week.

Almost all the work was done in this way—all by hand, with the help of animals.

The local workers were very diligent—and they were well paid by their standards. A laborer got eight-to-ten cents an hour. A carpenter got fifteen-to-twenty cents an hour. The workers lived on the site; they slept outside. For dinner, they would often heat up tomato sauce—and dunk bread into it.

Cement was the basis for everything. Like I said, we didn't have cranes or a cement-mixing plant, so we had to do it the old way. They would mix cement with sand and gravel and turn it over and over by shovel, and once it looked good they would shovel it into buckets and dump it into the forms. Then they'd add reinforcing steel, which would also be fabricated at the job site.

When we had to pour concrete on the upper level, they would build platforms and again they would proceed by mixing sand, gravel, cement and water and shovel it up from one level to the next, until they reached the area where it was going. At that point they would shovel the cement into buckets and pass it along in a human chain until it reached its destination.

It took a bit longer, but we got the job done. In fact, our site was visited by many professional people from Russia and France and other countries; they couldn't believe how beautiful our product was; and they marveled at how our system was far better than their system.

By the way, the locals thought we were crazy to use such beautiful plywood for concrete forms. They insisted that they would make furniture with this material and not concrete forms!

We also got the contract for another project at the University of Tunis—the Chott Maria Boarding School for students from six to seventeen years old.

With these two projects, our contract called for us to build dormitories, a dining hall, classrooms, an auditorium, roads and playgrounds.

We also had to put in a very large septic system with huge leeching fields—since no sewer system was available.

Speaking about sewer systems, the specifications called for the toilets to be a flat area, over which people would squat down and when they were finished they would pull a chain which would release water from a tank in the ceiling and it would flow down to the flat area and then flush everything out to the septic system. We had a hard time finding a supplier for this outdated system.

A couple of things stick in my mind from this time. One was that I hired a young man by the name of Moncef Aldari to be my interpreter and go-between with local people. I found him to be very honest and willing to learn our system.

Generally speaking, when I was in Tunis, I worked from morning to night, seven days a week. There was a lot I had to accomplish.

One day, to save a little time at lunch, I asked Moncef to go out and get us sandwiches.

His reply was, "What's a sandwich?"

I said, "Two pieces of bread with some meat or some cheese in between the bread."

Funny. A small world, yet still very different.

In Tunisia, like Europe, it's the custom that lunch consists of two or three hours, including a nap. To a fast-working American businessman, that's a big dent in each day!

My second interesting experience involved my meetings with subcontractors. I had to review their bids in the hope of getting them to reduce their original price to something less and also to be sure that they understood the work involved. Plus I had to determine if they were able to perform the work to everyone's satisfaction. Had they done similar work before? And if yes, then I asked for an explanation of how it was done and a description of the material that was used.

So when my translator and I met with the first subcontractor, I introduced myself as an American businessman. I thanked him for submitting his price for his work, and I said I was willing to give him a contract, but for a lesser amount.

He looked at me and got up and said, "Thank you for your time," and he left. I looked at my interpreter and said to him, "What the hell did you tell him?"

He looked at me and said, "Mr. Franchi, you have insulted him."

I asked him what that meant, and he said that I wasn't in America, I was in Tunisia. He said that I must use the local system.

I asked him what the hell the "local" system was, and he told me that it involved three steps. The first step was to meet and discuss your families. The second step was to discuss how you plan to perform the work. Finally, the third step was to meet and discuss the value of the work and the requirements of the specifications.

This was very painful to me since I didn't have that kind of time; but when in Rome, do what the Romans do.

I followed that suggestion and I met with the same gentleman again, and I was able to purchase his work for much less than what I had originally offered to him.

I had to do this with most of the other subcontractors. It was certainly painful to me—but it worked.

One other time, I asked my vice president, Bud O'Donnell, to take a trip with me to Tunis so he could get familiar with the site and the work procedures; the idea being that we could take turns traveling to Tunisia. We flew into Tunis on a Sunday. During our flight I had said that we needed to work really hard so we could leave on Friday morning, stop over in Rome to meet with the architect and then we'd rent a car and drive to Cortina to ski on Saturday and Sunday and leave that Monday morning for home. We didn't have too much choice in the matter, because there were no flights available after Friday afternoon for Rome. So we worked hard and long hours and we finished on time to fly to Rome and meet with the architect on Friday afternoon.

At the meeting, I asked the architect's secretary to do us a favor and to recommend an inn that we could stay at in Cortina. She did and we made a reservation. When we finished the meeting, Bud and I jumped into a taxi and I told the driver that I would give him a good tip if he could make it to the airport in time to catch our flight to Milano. We made it. But, my heart was hanging out since he drove on sidewalks and passed cars at a very high speed.

Anyway, I rented an automobile and drove to Cortina. We found our inn, but it was very late at night, actually very early in the morning, and the door to the inn was locked. When the innkeeper opened the door, we introduced ourselves and I asked him to bring us some prosciutto and cheese and wine, since we had not eaten anything since morning.

When we woke and looked out the window, we saw that it had snowed. We asked for a ski guide so we could go and rent our ski equipment and our ski clothes. They didn't rent clothes, so we had to ski in our business clothes. Each of us did purchase a wind breaker to use as a ski jacket.

The ski conditions were unbelievable and the people were really nice. Although they did keep pointing fingers at us—at our clothes—as if to say, "Look at those crazy Americans."

Our guide was a young man by the name of Anthony. We were having a great time. The conditions, the scenery and the weather were perfect. At noon, I wanted to keep on skiing, but Anthony said that we should stop and rest and have lunch, and that later we'd do more skiing.

I admit it was a more cosmopolitan way to ski.

So we did as he suggested and it was really great. Well, except for the end of the first day. It had really started to snow hard. Almost impossible to ski. Anthony put bells on his ski poles—so that we could follow him by listening to the bells and following the sound!

When we skied the next morning, in really beautiful weather, I saw how close we had come during the snow storm to the edge of a ravine. Without Anthony's bells, we could easily have plunged over the edge!

But all in all, we had two lovely days of skiing and a little bit of needed relaxation after working really hard in Tunisia.

Then it was time to go home. On Monday morning we went to a local airport to fly to Milano where we were scheduled to catch our flight for Boston. But the local plane flew between the mountains and, because it was cloudy, we had to wait for the clouds to dissipate. Finally, the skies were clear and we could fly. We flew between the Alps; the view was unbelievable—and very scary. Anyway, we made it to the Milano airport, but we just missed our flight home. So we decided to go to London, and from there we would get the next flight to Boston, the next morning. We sent a wire to our office letting them know what had happened and asking them to notify our families.

We made it home a day late. But that was the end of Bud O'Donnell going to Tunisia. He opted out, so, of course, I kept going back and forth until the work was completed.

My next venture was building a sizable project in Beirut, Lebanon, for American University. The work consisted of remodeling the existing nurses' quarters as well as remodeling many existing hospital wards. We also remodeled and built classrooms. We constructed an underground parking garage with a very large library above it.

I applied what I had learned in Tunisia; I did what the Romans did and stayed within their customs. We were moving along really well with the construction project; and my people who I had sent there were very happy—since Beirut is known as the Switzerland of the Middle East. It was a very popular vacation destination. Most people spoke English, and anything you could wish for was available. You could go snow skiing or swimming in the ocean. The weather was unbelievable and the food was wonderful.

Our construction work was moving really well—until one day when a civil war broke out. We were approximately 99 percent complete and the wives of my people who were working in Lebanon kept calling and asking, "Where is my husband? When is he coming home?"

I really could understand their concern, so I requested permission from the University to stop the work until the fighting stopped, since I couldn't get material to complete the work. And, also, my employees refused to go to the site.

Permission was not granted, so I decided that life was much more important and I brought back all of my employees, which made all the wives happy and my life at home much easier.

Unfortunately, the University canceled my contract and never paid the retainage—which was over a million dollars. Anyway, no lives were lost, and I've always felt that I made a donation to American University of one million dollars or more.

Still, back in Boston, many of the local contractors had come to me to obtain information about how they could bid work overseas. They saw the international market as a very lucrative venture. I told them the lessons that I learned in Tunisia—and that you need lots of passion—but don't lose your temper. It also helps to have a good interpreter who can tell you that you need to move in slow motion, as time is not important to these people because they enjoy the easy life.

While this was going on, I got an invitation from a Saudi prince to go to Saudi Arabia to look into the possibility of setting up a company in Riyadh. It was a long trip. I had a terrible time getting through customs at the airport, even though I had an invitation from a prince. Finally, I got to my hotel and checked in to find out that my room had window openings but no actual windows; there was nothing to shut and I could hear dogs barking all night long. I didn't sleep well at all.

In the morning, I met the prince for breakfast. Right away, he started dictating how this relationship would work. He would have 51 percent of the company and would tell me which projects to do and what fees I would be getting for my company. He indicated that we would get many projects and that, of course, I would be responsible for everything.

He was very arrogant and I knew I couldn't work with him—and I knew I didn't want to send my people into this kind of an arrangement. I wasn't going to give anyone 51 percent and I wasn't going to take orders from him.

I went home—and had another tough time getting through customs on the way out—and then I wrote the prince a nice but firm letter and said, "No thanks."

That was it for international business as far as I was concerned.

Tunisia was finished. Lebanon was in a civil war. And Saudi Arabia had an arrogant royal pain for a prince.

BUILDING MY LIFE

CHAPTER ELEVEN
Famiglia

All this work. All this traveling. It was very exciting. It was very successful, but it did put a strain on our family.

I'm very close to my own family. I've also always been close to my wife's family. Family is very, very important.

I made a point to visit my family once a week. And the same with my in-laws—usually for lunch. I often took my father and also my father-in-law to visit my construction sites. I even took them to Florida and Africa! One minor issue was that my father-in-law had a very bad snoring problem. But he loved to travel and see what I was doing, so I put up with the noise! My parents and my in-laws were wonderful people.

One day, when I was working in Tunis, I had a call from my wife. Madeline told me that our two oldest children, Linda and Debra—who were in high school—had skipped out of the house without Madeline's permission and had gone to a party at Boston University. They'd been invited by a boy, a friend of our family, who was a student at B.U.

I was so upset that I took the very next flight out of Tunis for home.

When I got home, I sat the girls down and told them how disappointed I was. How disappointed there mother was. And to do something like that when I was out of the country? In North Africa?

I punished my girls.

They were not permitted to go to any parties—for a whole year. I stuck to my guns, but I also realized at the same time that I shouldn't do any more huge projects so far away from home. I needed to be with my family.

I was, naturally, also upset with the young man who had invited my girls to the party without asking their mother for permission. I had a very long talk with the boy's parents; they fully understood my concerns and they apologized; but we never saw them again.

Oh, I also made my two daughters write, "I WILL NOT DO THIS AGAIN"—450 times each.

This may seem odd or even extreme to today's parents. But the way I look at it is this: You bring children into this world, you have a responsibility to give them a proper upbringing.

Both girls realized that I was right in my actions. In fact, we were very friendly after that. Problems often bring a sense of understanding. They understood that there are standards that we all have to live by. They also understood how much their mother and I cared for them.

So after that, any young escort who wanted to ask one of my daughters out had to come to me first!

I remember one young man who came to my house to ask to take Linda to a dance at the high school. His name was Jim. He appeared very sloppily dressed, and he had long hair and a scruffy beard.

I looked at this young man and I said to him, "Jim, before we talk, please go home, take a shower, shave, get a hair cut and put on clean clothes. Then come back and we'll talk."

I thought that I would never see Jim again. But guess what? The next day, Jim appeared again, nice and clean. I was glad to see him. I liked him. He had it rough. He was living with his grandmother, because his parents were not around. Anyway, we talked for a long time and finally I said he could take Linda to the dance, but he had to get her back home by 11:00 P.M. He became like a son to me. He was always at the house. He practically lived in our house—not just for Linda's sake, but he enjoyed talking to me and all my children. He needed love, which we gave.

Linda's sidekick, her sister Debra, was also a very attractive young lady. In fact she was crowned Queen of the Prom.

Linda and Debra dressed really nicely, but I bought all of their skirts and made sure they went a little below the knee. They were not really happy because all of their friends were wearing mini-skirts, which I didn't approve of for my girls. However, I found out later that all of the girls—Linda, Debra and Patty—when they reached the bus stop, would raise their skirts above their knees. Debra also brought home some strange young men and I took my time to interview each of them, rejecting a couple of them within minutes. There were a few I took my chances with—but spent the evenings pacing the floor until whoever was out got home safely.

An odd case was a young man who came to see me after he and Debra broke up. He asked me if I could help him pay for college! I told him he should apply for government loans. He did and, believe it or not, he's a doctor today.

I continued through this time to make a strong effort to do a lot together as a family. To take a lot of family trips.

This meant that I didn't have time for international travel.

Little did I know that everything was about to be taken out of my hands.

Because—like a bolt of lightning—my life changed in a flash.

CHAPTER TWELVE
The Light Fails

One day, my wife said she was not feeling well. It had been going on for a while. So we went for a check up. She was examined, and they ran a number of tests.

When all was done, the diagnosis was that Madeline had ovarian cancer.

I couldn't believe it.

My Madeline was sick. Very sick.

To this day—forty years later—it still seems so unbelievable.

She was very brave throughout the entire ordeal. It was a long fight. She suffered for several years. My children and I, of course, rallied round her—and each other.

We did all we could. We helped, we took turns going to doctor visits and treatment sessions.

It goes without saying that this is what every family does. Cancer doesn't just hit a particular person—it hits the family. And the family fights back.

So we did. So we tried. As hard as we thought possible.

You always think, after the fact, that you could have done more. Or made quicker decisions. Or better decisions. But—you know—you don't really make any decisions when it comes to cancer. Cancer makes the decisions for you. All you can do is stay strong. Stay on course. Stay with the fight.

It was a fight that Madeline lost. It was a fight that we all lost.

Madeline passed away at the age of 42. It was a terrible shock to me and to our families. I lost the love of my life. My children lost their mother.

I don't know what I would have done—if it hadn't been for the children.

We were blessed with six beautiful children.

So, right away, I cut back on my commitments. I closed the Florida office. I started phasing out the construction company—Franchi Construction Co., Inc.

I started concentrating on real estate ventures so that I could be local. So that I could be closer to my children.

I wanted to carry on, the way things had been.

Of course, nothing would ever be the same again, and it was all so much more terrible because we were a very tight family. We did almost everything together. We had a lot of wonderful traditions.

On Christmas Eve, we'd always invite the two families—my side and my wife's side—to our house. It was a great time. We'd put out a terrific spread—*after* we ate a great dinner!

Then everyone had to perform something—a song or a skit. We all participated. Then we'd all go to midnight mass. It was really wonderful.

Madeline missed a lot of those experiences.

She never saw her family grow up—she never saw her grandchildren become teenagers.

It was quite the kick in the gut.

But I had to rally. I had to rise to the challenge. I had to become a father and a mother.

I realized right away that I had to learn how to be more flexible. Before, if I had been too tough on one of the kids, then Madeline would soften the blow.

I knew that God had been good enough to give me six beautiful children. I knew I had a choice: Hire someone to watch my children, or do it myself. I decided that since we brought these wonderful children into this world, I should not turn them over to unknown people to be raised. So I decided it was my responsibility to raise my children and have them become good citizens and good people.

I decided to do it myself.

I phased out my construction business and became as much of a full-time father and mother as I could. It wasn't long before I had completely shut down the construction company.

An unforeseen ramification was that, as I phased out, owners began to stop paying me on a number of requisitions and extras. People who I had worked with for years, suddenly started giving me a hard time about paying me. They took advantage of my misfortune.

I had trouble paying my bills.

Many nights, I walked the streets at three or four in the morning—thinking, "How am I going to pay my bills?" All six kids would be asleep, and I couldn't sleep. So I'd go out for a walk. There was a coffee shop in Newton Corner that was open all night. I'd be in there at three in the morning, thinking about how to pay my bills.

Finally, I decided to call a meeting in my office with all my large creditors and explain to them my problem—that I was having a hard time collecting money from the owners for all the extra work I had done at their request, and that I also had problems collecting the very large retainage which they owed me becuase they knew I was going to close down my company and they thought they could put enough pressure on me to make me settle for less money.

I told my creditors that I would resist this unfair pressure and that was why I couldn't pay them at that moment.

"I promise you that I will pay you in full," I said, "but I ask that you all give me a little more time to work this out."

There was not one supplier or subcontractor who objected.

They said, "Pat, we know you well and we know you will stand by your words—so do what you need to do and pay us when you can."

Two suppliers—Michael Pirolli from M.J. Pirolli and Jr. Generagzio from New England Sand and Gravel—offered me blank checks and said to fill them out and pay them back when I could.

Tears came to my eyes. I will never forget this. This shows how you need to be fair, respectful and honest with people, just the way you would want to be treated yourself.

The conclusion was that I went ahead and sold three beautuful pieces of property, and I used those funds to pay those wonderful people who had faith in me.

Eventually, I received all the money owed me from the various owners, and that put me back in a good financial position.

The lesson here is: Be truthful and have faith in your fellow man.

Now, getting back to my family and how to handle all the responsibilities, I took the step of hiring a housekeeper to help with cooking and cleaning.

A very nice older woman from Trinidad named Ina. She was with us for years and became like part of the family. The kids loved her. If we went somewhere on vacation, the kids would always say, "We have to get a gift for Ina."

On Christmas Eves, when the family did our little skits, Ina would dress up in exotic costumes and would dance and sing. She really enjoyed it. Everyone loved her. She would win first prize.

Eventually, she moved into a little apartment we set up for her in the basement. She'd stay at our house during the week, but she would go into Boston every weekend to be with her relatives. One weekend, as a surprise, we decided to replace all of her furniture. We bought new chairs and a couch and set it all up, and we gave the old stuff to a very nice and very honest man who worked for me for many years.

Well, on Saturday, that man who had taken the furntiure called me —Ina was still away—and said that under the cushions he had found a bunch of money!

"Did you hide the money while playing poker?" he said.

What had happened was that Ina had been saving what I paid her in cash and put it in a cushion in the chair. The guy was an honest person and called me and we got the money back.

But—and I admit that this was a little devilish of me—when I picked up Ina on Monday morning at the bus station, which I did every week, she asked how my weekend had been.

"Not so good, Ina," I answered.

"What happened?" she asked.

"Well. Someone ransacked our house," I said. "They stole all of the furniture out of your apartment!"

Ina was a black woman, but she turned white.

"Don't worry," I said. "I went out and bought you new furniture."

She started to cry.

Okay, I had gone too far.

I told her the truth and she regained her composure and was very happy. She was also very happy with her new furniture.

But—I told her to open a bank account, and I took her to the bank to make sure she did it.

All went well until several years later when she decided to return to Trinadad. She was really a wonderful person and to this day we still talk about her—how wonderful she was and how she helped so much with the children.

I really believe that Madeline had something to do in finding Ina for us!

CHAPTER THIRTEEN
With Six, You Coach Little League

Six children.

What's a guy to do?

Become a Little League coach for one thing.

That was one of the best times in my life. I coached my son's team —11 to 12 children—and we did a pretty good job. We had lots of practices. I loved baseball and understood the game somewhat. And, I guess I had a knack for teaching the kids.

I told them that they must work hard to win—that nothing comes easy. My team practiced the most of any team. It apparently worked, because we won more games each year than any other team and we made the playoffs every year. I guess I showed them a little something about having a vision.

Also, I promised them that if they won the game, I'd take them all for ice cream. But if they lost, they had to run ten laps around the field.

I don't know how that would go over with parents today—when every kid gets a trophy for just showing up. The kids responded, however. They enjoyed playing and wanted to do their best. What's wrong with that?

We worked together as a team.

The only thing I asked the parents to do was to drop off the kids at the field and then pick them up when we were finished. I'd handle everything else. The parents had a schedule of carpooling that worked well. The kids would get dropped off; I'd run practice; the kids would get picked up.

There was one day when the designated parents didn't show up. This was before cell phones. So what could I do? I had twelve kids and my daughter Susanne who was my assistant coach—and I was driving a two-seater Mercedes.

I looked at the kids and said, "Hop in."

Somehow, they all managed to squeeze in and I drove everyone home. Thankfully, no police saw me doing that.

At the end of each season, I'd take the team to Fenway for a Red Sox game.

That was a lot of fun.

I remember ordering thirteen of things. The vendors would walk up and down the aisles and I'd yell out, "Thirteen hot dogs!" Then, "Thirteen popcorns!" Then, "Thirteen ice creams!" That was funny. And enjoyable.

My daughter Susanne was my assistant coach. She's the female athlete in the family. She had a knack—even back then—for organization. She kept track of everything: practice schedules, batting orders, pitcher rotations. She'd sit next to me on the bench and keep things going the way they were supposed to go.

At the end of each season, we also had a team cookout at my house. And the kids would try and grab me and throw me into our swimming pool. I climbed a tree to escape them. They gave up and when I came down I got a bucket of water and turned the tables on them!

CHAPTER FOURTEEN
To the Slopes—and Beyond

My children and I also did a lot of traveling. We became a skiing family. We all loved to ski. We still do.

One weekend, three of my daughters and I had planned a trip to Killington in Vermont. I got home after work on Friday and we were all rushing to leave. No dinner. We jumped into the car and off we went to our weekend ski trip.

In Vermont, I pulled over to buy gas.

No wallet!

I had changed clothes in a hurry and left my wallet in my work clothes!

I looked at the kids and said, "Anyone have any money?"

Patty said, "I have ten dollars."

I bought five dollars worth of gas and kept driving.

At the hotel, I asked to speak to the manager and I explained to him what had happened. I told him that if he could help us out, I'd send him a check as soon as I got home.

"What do you need?" he asked.

"Well, everything."

I needed two rooms. I needed money for lift tickets. I needed cash for meals.

He looked at me and asked if I had any identification.

"Only my three kids," I answered.

He gave me everything I asked for.

And the minute I got home, I wrote a check and mailed it.

I learned then that it's always better to give someone the benefit of the doubt.

Sometimes you get stuck, but most of the time it works out okay. And it just makes you feel better about life to trust people.

We didn't just ski.

One year we all went to the Grand Canyon. Wow. That was something. We flew in and got to the lodge that we were going to leave from on our expedition. We got food and equipment and tents and such, and we sailed out in rubber rafts.

The scenery was just unbelievable.

The first night—remembering that a friend had been on this trip and had said that it never rains in the desert—we didn't set up the tents. We put out our sleeping bags and laid on our backs gazing up at the stars. There's no light pollution. You can see everything. Every star. It was as amazing as the Grand Canyon. And we didn't have to worry about rain because we were in a desert.

Naturally, it started to rain. To pour!

We grabbed the tent and tried to set it up, but it was a disaster and so we just sort of put it over us to keep dry. We were wet and we were laughing our heads off.

It was a great seven days. Together. All of us. A beautiful family get-together. Nearly every trip we made, we all went together. I made sure of that. We did it for ourselves. And we did it for Madeline.

We really enjoyed skiing out west because conditions were better. No ice. The people were much more helpful. No one would cut the lines. No one would step on your skis.

One year, when I had planned one of these west-coast ski trips, I made reservations and paid for everything. But the weather looked bad. They had no snow. It got to be close to the time when I could still cancel everything and get my money back. So that's what I did. Then we shifted gears, and I booked a different trip—to the west coast of Florida.

We went to Sanibel Island and we had a great time. We fell in love with the area. It seemed like a family resort. Lots of things to do—and all of it was good clean family fun.

I saw a condo site under construction. So I stopped in and checked it out. I liked what I saw and we loved the area—so I bought a unit.

For a long time, we made yearly trips.

We also still loved skiing.

We were die-hard skiers; we started at Black Mountain, a family-oriented mountain in Jackson, New Hampshire.

Then we graduated to Cranmore, a more challenging mountain in North Conway.

Later we started going to Wildcat, in Pinkham Notch. Wildcat was my favorite of all the mountains in New Hampshire.

We went to Vermont sometimes, but we liked New Hampshire the best. I remember one of our weekend trips to Waterville Valley, in New Hampshire; it was three of my daughters and me. When we arrived, one of the girls, Debra I believe, announced that she had left her suitcase at home with all her ski clothes. So, guess what? I had to purchase her an entirely new outfit. I think she did it purposefully, so that she'd look good on the ski trails.

Anyway, we were spending a lot of time in New Hampshire; we skied at Wildcat; and in the summers I always attended the Volvo tennis tournaments that were held at Mt. Cranmore.

So I got to thinking about maybe buying a mountain!

I set my sights on Mt. Cranmore. The Mt. Cranmore ski resort and the Mt. Cranmore tennis club were owned by different people, and I had heard that the Mt. Cranmore tennis club might be auctioned off. I also had heard that the owners of the Mt. Cranmore ski resort might be willing to sell sometime later on.

I thought it would be good to purchase the tennis club and then later, when the mountain was going to be sold, I would try to purchase it as well and bring it all under one ownership.

Sure enough, the tennis club was put up for auction—and I bought it. A while later, Cranmore decided to sell the ski mountain, as I had predicted. I met with one of the owners, the man who was managing the ski area at that time. After several meetings, we agreed to a purchase price and we both had our lawyers write up a purchase-and-sale agreement that both parties were to sign. On the specified date, my lawyer and I went to the meeting to sign the purchase-and-sale agreement, but an hour later the Cranmore attorney showed up and indicated that he was instructed by the manager that the mountain was not going to be sold. I was very disappointed, but that's life.

However, I found out later that the owner who had been negotiating with me had also been negotiating with another potential buyer and that the owner reneged on my deal because the other buyer had assured that owner that he'd have a job at Cranmore as a manager, guaranteed for several years.

Again, I was very upset, because the owner had been playing a game with me. He knew very well that I was not going to offer him a job, because, quite frankly, he was a poor manager.

Because of his actions, I went out and purchased as much land around Cranmore that I could get my hands on, so that the new owners couldn't expand or build any housing.

At that point, I happened to learn that Wildcat Mountain was having financial difficulties. This was good timing. I looked at the mountain and after many meetings an agreement was reached. This time it worked!

I bought Wildcat. I took it over and paid off all the outstanding debts to a number of vendors. Then I began to upgrade all the equipment and ski trails. I built a brand-new lodge. I constructed and installed the fastest detachable chairlift in New England, by replacing the old two-seat gondolas that were very slow.

Here's an odd bit of history. We took down the old gondolas which the previous owners had purchased from Italy and auctioned them off. A certain woman at the auction bid very high on one particular gondola. So I approached her and asked her why she wanted it. She replied that was where she had conceived her first child! That blew my mind—and I couldn't figure out how that could be accomplished in such a tight space, not to mention that both people would have been all bundled up in ski clothes. I guess that where there's a will, there's a way.

It took a lot of capital to get Wildcat going again. But it was fun—taking a dying cat and returning it to a roaring life.

I did it because I had a vision. As it turned out, it was the worst vision I ever had!

Well, it was okay I guess.

But owning a ski resort isn't easy. Everything is dependent on the weather and you can't control the weather!

If there was no snow, you had to make snow.

Then if it rained, the snow washed away and you had to make it again.

If it was windy, you had to shut down the ski lifts—and people would ask for their money back and go to other mountains.

I wasn't involved on a daily basis; I hired a manager. But I kept up with it and did spend a fair amount of time there.

Wind. Rain. Snow.

You can't manage wind, rain and snow.

Still, I kept it for twenty-two years.

After that though, the kids were older and didn't always want to go. And I realized that, for myself, it was easier to put on a pair of golf shoes than it was to put on ski boots. So I finally sold it.

CHAPTER FIFTEEN
Goals

This may seem hard to believe, but for me all these ventures were never about the money. Yes, I wanted to be successful and get rewarded for the time and effort I put in. But when you come down to it, I love simple things. I love accomplishing things. The money doesn't really mean anything. Money, to me, is just a tool I use to work with.

I think my family was proud of what I did, or of what I have accomplished. I felt it was just my daily routine.

I didn't talk about it too much with my parents, because it was just what my job was, and I loved what I was doing.

Other people would say that they were driving to Boston to check out a job there. I said that I was flying to North Africa to check out a job there. It didn't seem like anything special to me. It was another trip to someplace that I had an interest in—a place that I was building for the future. It was a place where I met new and different people with different outlooks on life. And always, it would be a place with new challenges.

I took my father to Tunisia once. And I knew he was impressed.

I took my father-in-law to Cape Canaveral a couple of times and he thought it was pretty amazing—but he snored too much! He snored so much that finally, on my second trip with him, I took my own room so that I could function the next day. But he was good company and I enjoyed having him with me.

After my father retired, I could see that he was bored.

So, I said, "Why don't you go to my job site and keep an eye on what's going on and we'll pay you a weekly salary."

"When?" he replied.

"Tomorrow," I said. "I will have somebody pick you up and I will show you a hospital that I'm building—along with several barracks and the dining hall."

Again, he never said much, but he loved going to sites. He couldn't wait to be picked up every morning. I knew he was proud of me. And that meant a lot.

I had a vision. To build a company that built things that I would be proud of—that would leave a good taste with the owners and be an example of very good workmanship.

I'd stay up at night and wonder, "How can I accomplish this goal?"

I'd wonder how I could be more competitive against other contractors? But without cheating on material or good workmanship.

It all involves good leadership and a good working crew. Without a good crew, you can't accomplish the goals that you have set for yourself. You need to let the crew know how much you appreciate the work they've produced. It's important that you pat a person on the shoulder when it's appropriate.

A lot of times, that's even more important than money. Because a compliment comes from the heart. It doesn't cost anything. But its value is immeasurable.

At the end of the day, everyone has to be proud that they accomplished a goal—that they had a good productive day.

No matter what type of skill you have, it's important that you feel that you have given it all you have. That's true of people who work with their hands or of people who work in offices or of people who act in movies or of people who play professional sports.

How many times do you see a game on TV and think that a particular athlete is just going through the motions? And getting paid millions?

That's why when I had a worker who did a great job—who was getting paid a lot less than millions—I always wanted to let him or her know that it was a good job and that I appreciated it.

That's how I wanted to be treated.

That's why I had goals.

And I went for it.

It's that simple.

BUILDING MY LIFE

CHAPTER SIXTEEN
Tradition

The bad part started with my wife's diagnosis. My wife, my children, our family—our life changed forever after that.

At this point, as I've said before, I had to make a major decision. Should I hire a nanny to raise my children and continue with my construction company, or should I be the person to be there to see my children grow up and become good people? The decision was easy. I decided that if I had been blessed with six wonderful children, then it would be me and not an outsider who would take care of them and see them mature and be an ongoing part of their lives.

So—the decision was made. I was going to cut back at work.

I had 650 employees. As we scaled back, I began laying off people. That was really hard. A lot of these people had worked for me for many years. We still had a number of projects that were ongoing, so the scaling-back took place over three or four years. I had to let people go when a job was finished.

But they found new jobs without a problem. Other contractors knew that people who worked for me were good people and did great work. That made me feel a little better.

In fact, just three or four years ago, we had a reunion. About 75 people came. From all over the country. Many flew in for the occasion. I hadn't seen most of them for thirty years! It was great. We had a wonderful dinner and talked and caught up on everyone's lives.

As for my own life, I had to make some big changes.

Madeline passed away on April 29, 1974. As I've said, I decided to concentrate my time on raising my family. My first rule was that we would do things together. If you let it slip, before you know it, not everyone makes every event. It wasn't easy for the family, but I insisted that we do things together.

So, how do you manage six kids on a day-to-day basis?

My answer is that if you can manage 650 employees, you can manage 6 kids.

We had a lot of family meetings. I made sure everyone knew what they were doing and what they had to do. And what I had to do. I made sure we were all heading in the right direction.

I was really proud of my children and wanted everyone to know. On Easter, my kids—especially the girls—were the best-dressed kids. After church, I'd drive with my children to visit all my relatives—to show off my kids. Everyone loved seeing us. They came to expect it, and they would call if we were late, to see if anything had happened.

I enjoyed taking my girls shopping for clothes. It was a formal affair. We'd go to Lord & Taylor and the clerks would put us in a private room. Models would come in wearing all different kinds of clothes and we'd pick out outfits for all the girls.

My son Michael was only eight years old when Madeline died. It hit him very hard, as you might expect. He slept with me every night until he was fourteen.

Finally, I said, "You really can't do this anymore."

It was sad, but, you know, it had to be done.

One night I saw him sneaking into the doorway of my bedroom. He had those sad eyes.

"Come on," I said. "Just for tonight."

He and I were very close when he was growing up.

I was close with all my kids and wanted them to do well. All of them were involved in sports. Sports are good for kids. Keeps them busy. Keeps them off drugs. Keeps them out of trouble. It also is great for them in terms of healthy living—and they make great friends.

So, all in all, we got through it. They turned out to be pretty good kids and adults.

One thing that we concentrated on, I guess because we're Italian, was meals.

Meals are the most important thing, when you think about it. The family gets together, at the same table at the same time. We eat. We talk. We laugh. We cry.

I kept up the tradition of the big Sunday dinner. And during the week, we had dinner every night at 6:00 P.M.

For Sunday, we had a classic, Italian, multi-course dinner. There was always spaghetti and meatballs. There would be a chicken or beef course. Sometimes I'd make stuffed lamb. There were always lots of vegetables. And, because we're not a dessert family, there was always a variety of fruit.

I did most of the cooking myself. I never liked cooking all that much—but, hey, you've got to cook—it's survival. I started cooking way back when we lived in Italy. My mother and my older brothers would be working out in the fields, and my mother would ask me to do lunch for them. I was probably ten years old. So I'd put things together. Sandwiches. Meats. Cheese. Bread. I'd put together a good lunch and bring it out to them in the field. They told me that it all tasted very good. When you are hungry, everything tastes good! I always had a good feeling for the kitchen.

So I'd cook for the kids and me. Once Ina came on board, she'd do some of the cooking. In fact we'd compete. One Thanksgiving, she said she could cook a better turkey! So we had a contest; each of us cooked a turkey. My turkey won, hands down. From then on, we went back to having just one turkey—my turkey!

An interesting thing about Thanksgiving is that we went American all the way. That's what my mother had done and what Madeline had done. Some Italian families try to add Italian dishes to the menu. But we didn't. It was a classic American meal: turkey, stuffing, vegetables, pumpkin pie. My stuffing got me a quizzing every year. What's in it? I wouldn't tell them. They didn't like it that much—but it gave off an aroma that made Thanksgiving official.

I've got to tell you something about our weekday dinners.

After dinner, we would hold a court trial at the table. We'd go around the table and talk about what each child had done that day—at school, at home. If someone had done something that was a problem—had done something wrong—then we'd have a trial. Evidence was given. Explanations. Reasons.

Then, we'd vote the penalty and the court would decide what the sentence would be. It kept everyone on their toes. It kept everyone interested. It helped me with parenting—but it was also a way to stay close and to have fun together. Oh—who do you think was the judge? Me, of course.

We were living in Weston, Massachusetts, when all this happened. We moved from our first house in Newton to Weston in 1963.

Madeline didn't want to move to Weston. She thought it was at the edge of civilization. And she almost got her wish.

But I kept telling her how beautiful it would be to bring up our children out in the country—and yet to also be not far from our family. We'd have more open space. More privacy. And, I said she'd be able to do many things that we couldn't do in Newton, such as having horses.

We did get horses. We had three of them and the girls would take them to horse shows. We had one horse that kept getting out. We had neighbors calling us; we had police in Weston and Wellesley call us.

"Are you missing a horse?"

One morning my wife got a call from a neighbor who was really fussy in keeping his lawn in great shape—it's not a stretch to say that he manicured his lawn. The night before it had rained quite a bit and, as always happens, our horses decided to go onto his lawn and they made quite the mess on the wet grass. He was really mad, and started yelling at my wife. He said he wanted to talk to me, and Madeline told him that I was in Tunisia! He calmed down at that and he apologized to her for yelling.

So, a couple of years later, early on a cold November morning, that same man called and said that our horses were in his yard again. I ran over with a couple of apples to induce the horses to come to me, which they did.

At that moment I said that I had had enough with horses. And I knew that the girls at this point were more interested in boys; so they didn't mind when I found another home for the horses.

But, let me back up a bit. We got into Weston because I found a sub-division that was under construction in a beautiful location; it was very near the Wellesley line.

I finally convinced Madeline that it was the time to move to Weston. So I approached the broker who was selling the land. We negotiated a price, and I signed the agreement and put a deposit down on this land.

Next thing I knew, I got the check back with a letter telling me that I was rejected—because I was Italian.

I was very disappointed and hurt, but I was not going to stop there, since I had worked very hard to convince my wife to move to Weston.

I went to a friend of mine who was building houses on speculation in Weston, and I asked him if he would sell me one lot. Which he did. It wasn't as good as the original location, but I wasn't going to be kept out because of my heritage.

Imagine that. I had served in the Marines, and some people thought I wasn't good enough to live in Weston.

While this was happening, the original broker called several months later and said that that the original land was suddenly available if I wanted it. I have no idea what happened. But I had to decide whether to swallow my pride or tell them to go to Hell.

I decided to look at the long run. I bought that land, plus an additional lot, because I knew it would be a great location for us.

My wife and I designed our dream house, based on our needs and around our family's needs. We had a great time doing it.

We had all kinds of ideas about how the rooms should be placed and where things would go. There were a million details, of course. It was all a great deal of satisfaction—and fun. I built the house myself—with the help of my father who did all the masonry work and the stone walls.

So—business was going well, our family was expanding and we had moved into our dream house in Weston.

The house was quite large and with six children it kept my beautiful wife quite busy. She was the type who wanted to do everything herself: housework, prepare lunch for the children, make dinner for the whole family, do laundry and all the other jobs a house has. I kept telling her to get some help. But Madeline kept on saying that would take too much time away from her because she would have to pick up the person at the bus stop, make lunch for her and give her a ride back to the bus line. Therefore, she felt it was too much wasted time.

One day when I came home from work, I found Madeline on her hands and knees scrubbing the kitchen floor. At that point, I really got mad at her and I said that I had married a wonderful lady and I never wanted to see her on her knees again. So what did I do?

The very first thing I did the next day was to contact an agency that specialized in bringing in mother's helpers from South America and I chose a young lady from Brazil. Her name was Angelina, but we always called her Angela. After the agency did a background check on me, I signed a contract for one year to have Angela live with us and help my wife with the daily chores. However, I never told my wife what I had done! So thirty days later I was notified by the agency that Angela was coming in on such-and-such a day on such-and-such a flight and I was to meet her at Logan Airport. Now I got really concerned about how I was going to handle this. So I met Angela at the airport at around 6:00 P.M. She had one suitcase and she got into my car and here we go! What was I going to say to Madeline? I had been thinking about this since the agency informed me that Angela was coming. Well, I reached home and I opened the back door to the house and we walked into the kitchen. Madeline was making dinner. Angela was walking behind me.

Before Madeline could say anything, I came up with a story.

"I was at the airport, and I found this young lady who was looking to be a mother's helper, and I decided to take her home to help you so that you will never be on your knees again scrubbing floors."

I got an evil eye from my wife.

"Where will she stay?" Madeline asked.

"Oh. She can sleep on the couch today, and then we'll make a permanent space for her."

After a few days, everyone was happy and Angela and Madeline became very good friends.

Eventually, Angela decided to go to night school to learn English, and after the end of her contract she went to work with another family in Weston. She met a gentleman from Weston and got married and guess what? After a few years, she went ahead and hired a mother's helper!

You never know what tomorrow will bring.

After Angela left, we continued to bring in mother's helpers until such time that our children went to college. And at that time we had day help as needed.

Again, the lesson is that one needs to take action.

The Weston house is where we still live today. I've put the house and land in trust, hoping that someday one of my great-grandchildren will want to live there and keep the tradition going.

After all, a homestead is a homestead.

From Gallinaro to Weston—it's really the same home, just in a few different places.

PAT FRANCHI

*On the following pages are photographs of my life—
of Italy, of America—
of my work through the years—
and, most of all, of my family.*

*They bring back memories that make me proud,
that make me sad, that make me happy.*

*Mostly—they are memories of appreciation
for all the blessings I've had.*

Gallinaro, Italy. The home where I was born.

We were certainly well out in the country. It was a good, simple, sturdy house. Notice the vineyard in front—where my mother's great wine got its start.

PAT FRANCHI

*Our passport photo to go
to the New World!*

*That's my mother, Giovanna, on the left. I'm standing in
back. And there's my sister Maria
and my little brother Anthony.*

*I was the only one who didn't get sick
on the voyage across the Atlantic.*

My father, Luigi Franchi, in America.

He loved smoking his pipe and relaxing in his yard. Which was wonderful, but it made me avoid hiring pipe smokers!

He was an excellent bocce player. I really enjoyed the times we had playing together. Of course, he wasn't happy if I was the captain of the other team and threw the boccino as far as I could!

My mother, Giovanna Franchi.

She was the driving force behind our family. If she wanted something, she went for it. I think I inherited that attitude from her. I hope I did.

Semper Fi.

*I was very proud to serve my new country as a member of the Marine Corps.
Here I am, right after basic training, before shipping out to Midway.*

PAT FRANCHI

My wonderful wife Madeline.

*This was taken at a fundraiser
for the Boys & Girls Club.*

*Madeline loved her family and she loved helping
others. She was the light of our lives.*

*Here I am, the eager businessman,
trying to follow my vision.*

PAT FRANCHI

My beautiful daughers—
Linda (on the left) and Debra.

They're ready for a formal dance in high school.
Of course, any young man had to ask me for
permission before going out
with one of my daughters.

BUILDING MY LIFE

My daughter Patty and me, skiing at Lake Tahoe.

And this is Patty when she was a volunteer for our cancer-research endowment at Dana-Farber Hospital.

PAT FRANCHI

Susanne was a great athlete—and helped me coach little league. Notice her trophies.

BUILDING MY LIFE

*My two sons—Michael, age 9,
and Louie, age 15,
posing with my sister, their Aunt Maria.*

PAT FRANCHI

Here I am, coaching my son Michael in little league. Notice how overjoyed he is.

And below is the whole team, with my amazing assistant coach—my daughter Susanne.

BUILDING MY LIFE

This is my wonderful friend Fran and me, enjoying a day at the beach at Sanibel Island in Florida.

Fran and I have traveled on great trips to Italy, Spain, Scotland, Australia, New Zealand, Egypt, Paris and the beaches of Normandy.

Below is the amazing Basilica of the Holy Family in Barcelona, designed by Antoni Gaudi.

PAT FRANCHI

Three generations!

That's me, Fran, my grandson Austin, and Austin's father, my son Louie, at a golf tournament.

Nothing is more important than family. We've tried very hard over the years to do things together. And those times leave me with very wonderful and special memories.

My buddy, Spike.

Spike is a German Pinscher. He is my faithful friend, who keeps me company at all times. He is there saying goodbye to me each morning, and he welcomes me home each evening.
He is truly loyal to me.

Notice that his ears aren't cropped. I made an appointment to do it, but when I was walking into the vet with him, Spike gave me such a sad look that I turned right around and took him home!

Yahoo!

We've had great times with the kids and the snow at our Yahoo Weekends at Wildcat Mountain for families with children who have cancer.

Above, we're giving kids ski-mobile rides.

At left, a new skier having fun!

BUILDING MY LIFE

Are we having fun?
Yes!

There's plenty going on indoors as well!

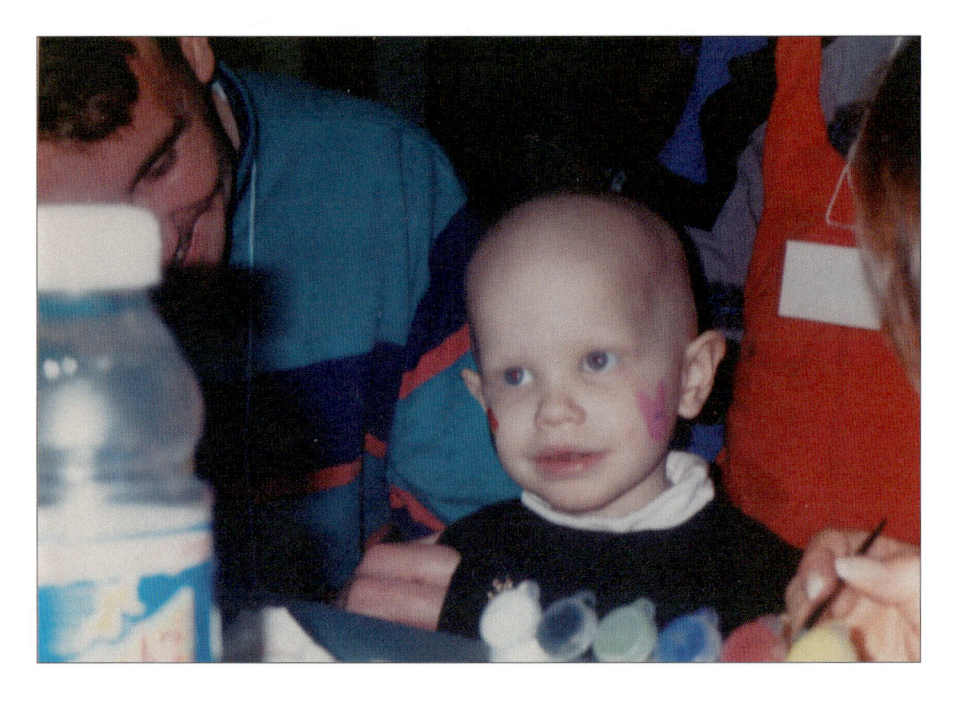

BUILDING MY LIFE

The wide view.

And the narrow view.

It's all fun!

PAT FRANCHI

The Jimmy Fund®
DANA-FARBER CANCER INSTITUTE

10 Brookline Place West, 8th Floor
Brookline, Massachusetts 02445-7226
(800) 52.JIMMY, 617.632.4070 fax
www.jimmyfund.org

January 23, 2014

Mr. Pasquale Franchi
16 Westcliff Road
Weston, MA 02493

Dear Pat,

It is my pleasure to recognize your continued commitment to Dana-Farber Cancer Institute and the Jimmy Fund. We are so grateful to have such wonderful partners in the Franchi family.

Since the Madeline Franchi Ovarian Cancer Research Fund was established in 2004, you have raised more than $1,900,000 in support of research into ovarian cancer under the direction of Dr. Ursula Matulonis, the Medical Director of the Susan F. Smith Center for Women's Cancers at Dana-Farber. This funding has enabled her team to conduct groundbreaking research and initiate new clinical trials.

You also graciously support research and clinical breakthroughs into pediatric oncology through the Susanne Marie Franchi Research Fund in Pediatric Oncology. Since the fund was established in 1983, you've raised more than $757,000 for research into childhood cancers, which has helped fuel new discoveries in treatment and care, numerous clinical trials, and new technologies.

In addition to the funds you established, you purchased a gene in our Gene Display to honor the Dana-Farber staff who cared for your family members and you've made numerous contributions to the Boston Marathon® Jimmy Fund Walk.

Your daughter, Patty Franchi Flaherty, also followed in your philanthropic footsteps. She was a member of the Dana-Farber Board of Trustees for 18 years and established two funds of her own.

Pat, your philanthropic commitment to research and patient care here at Dana-Farber ensures that Susanne and Madeline's memories will continue to be honored. You've taken two very difficult losses and turned them into an incredible family legacy that will continue to have a significant impact on our research and the lives of our patients for many years to come.

From everyone here at Dana-Farber Cancer Institute, thank you again for all that you do. We truly could not do this work without the support of you and your family.

Sincerely,

Suzanne Fountain

Suzanne Fountain
Assistant Vice President
Director, The Jimmy Fund

DANA-FARBER
CANCER INSTITUTE

A letter from Dana-Farber, thanking our foundations for raising more than $2.6 million for cancer research.

JOAN WALLACE-BENJAMIN, Ph.D.
President & CEO

January 16, 2014

Mr. Pasquale Franchi
182 W Central Street Ste 303
Natick, MA 01760-3756

Dear Pat,

It gives me great pleasure to write to you on the occasion of your autobiography to let you know what a wonderful friend you have been to The Home for Little Wanderers for so long. We were honored to acknowledge this friendship publicly at our annual luncheon for Cornerstone members, those giving to The Home for 20 years or more.

Your philanthropic generosity which, as I'm sure you know, now totals well over half a million dollars, has allowed us to provide so many benefits and "extras" to the children in our care — things that many families take for granted but which are not possible without support such as yours. Your participation in our Capital Campaign to rebuild Longview Farm was a leadership gift that set the tone for others and it makes me so proud to see your family's name commemorated on the gymnasium at Longview.

But your contributions to our work go well beyond your ability to help us financially. The time you have spared to see our programs at work – at the Children's Community Support Collaborative, the Southeast Campus in Plymouth, the Therapeutic After School Program, and our old facilities at Orchard House and Spring Park Place — is remembered with gratitude by us all, especially the children and staff. And then there were the fun times: the educational field trips, the Wildcat Ski Resort excursion and the golfing events.

Pat, it all adds up to a treasure trove of generosity that is difficult to put into words and even more difficult to adequately express thanks for. But, please know you have made a huge difference in the lives of so many children who come to us for help; many have suffered traumatic pasts and been through things no child should ever experience. Many of them have little hope when they get here, and few reasons to believe that anyone is on their side. Your actions go a long way to changing that belief.

We are most grateful to you.

Sincerely,

Joan Wallace-Benjamin, Ph.D.

271 Huntington Avenue, Boston, MA 02115 • tel. 617-267-3700 • 888-HOME-321 • fax. 617-267-8142 • www.thehome.org

A letter from
The Home for Little Wanderers,
thanking me for
"a treasure trove of generosity."
But, like I say, we're all in this together.

Boston's historic Vendome Hotel.

Rennovating this classic architectural gem was one of my best accomplishments—until that terrible tragedy—the fire that cost nine firemen their lives—marred it for me forever.

BUILDING MY LIFE

The Mass Pike Apartment Complex in Boston.

This was the site where one of the huge concrete slabs used for the exterior walls fell from a crane and smashed into bits. That turned out to be very lucky indeed, because we saw that the concrete fabricator had failed to add reinforcing rods. We had to have all of them completely redone, but we were fortunate to find out at the beginning of the project. The complex is fully occupied and is doing quite well.

PAT FRANCHI

Our office building in Chestut Hill.

*This is a very nice office space,
with retail shops on the first floor.*

*The Farm Project Apartment Complex
in Brookline Village. This was our biggest residential
construction project. It has more than 600 apartments,
plus a number of amenities, including a beautiful
swimming pool, underground parking and pleasant
tree-lined sitting areas. It has views of the Jamaica
Way, Leverett Pond and Olmsted Park. Notice that the
windows are not lined up with each other. This gives
the building an interesting, fluid look.*

Jamaica Way Apartments in Boston.

Located on the beautiful Jamaica Way, which winds its way into Boston, this complex has wonderful views of the city or Jamaica Pond.

BUILDING MY LIFE

Oliver Ames High School in Easton, Massachusetts.

This very modern school has a great deal of wonderful amenities, including a professional-level theater complex.

PAT FRANCHI

*Southeastern Massachusetts Technological Instiute,
North Dartmouth, Massachusetts.*

Designed by renowned architect Paul Rudolf, this classroom building looks like a wild sailing ship, with concrete and glass elements coming out of the edifice at all angles and directions. It is concrete in motion. I took my daughter Linda to the opening ceremonies and I asked her what she thought of the design, and she replied that she thought it reminded her of an octopus.

BUILDING MY LIFE

Apartment complex in St. Louis.

You do a good job and people talk good about you. I was asked by my bonding company if I was interested in completing a very sizable apartment complex in St. Louis, Missouri. The project had gone bust. I said yes, and we took over the job. I went in, figured out what went wrong and what had to be done. Four years later, I finished it. The developers were very pleased with the outcome.

The Federal Building in Burlington, Vermont.

I was very pleased with this sizeable project. Among other offices, it houses a courthouse and a post office.

The Charles River Arcade in Dedham, Massachusetts.

A large mall with very ample parking.

Working in Tunisia.

*We built the University of Tunis,
and, on the same campus, we also built
the Chott Maria Boarding School.*

*We constructed classrooms, dorms, dining rooms
and administration buildings.*

*And we did it almost entirely by hand! Donkeys were used to
carry dirt away from excavations, and concrete was mixed
by shovel and moved in buckets.*

Tunis adventure!

This is the law school, which included dorms, classrooms, a dining hall and an auditorium.

Considering I could speak neither Arabic nor French, I think it all worked out pretty well.

On our way to the moon!

*This is the engine-testing building we put up
at Cape Canaveral. The engines were tested inside,
before being attached to the rockets.*

NASA's rocket-assembly building.

Notice the huge doors. The entire rocket—standing upright—would be rolled out on a moving platform and taken to the launch tower.

NASA's administration building.

Perhaps the most intriguing space we built inside this complex housed the offices of Werner Von Braun. Known as the "Father of Rocket Science," Von Braun developed rockets in Germany during World War II. After the war, he and other scientists were secretly taken to the United States —and went to work on our rocket programs. His biggest triumph, of course, was to lead the team responsible for the giant Saturn V rocket—that blasted the Apollo missions into space and, eventually, to the moon.

BUILDING MY LIFE

We have lift off!

A Mercury rocket blasts off from Launch Tower #14. We were faced with the daunting task of redoing all the faulty welds and getting the tower up and operational in time for the first launch. We did it.

My official NASA identification badge.

*I saw the opportunity of a lifetime in Cape Canaveral,
and I went down and set up an office
and looked for a chance to get involved.
That's one decision I'll never regret.*

BUILDING MY LIFE

You can't do anything without vision.

This photograph was taken at the groundbreaking ceremony for Cabot Estates.

Whether it was land or buildings, in this country or on the other side of the world, I always had a vision of what I wanted to accomplish. Of course, my family is the vision I remain most proud of.

CHAPTER SEVENTEEN
My Kids

There's no other way to do this, other than to simply do it in order. Let me start with Linda, our oldest.

She was born on December 5, 1952.

Linda was a very elegant young lady. She had wonderful manners and a calm disposition. She was the peacemaker in the family. That's usually the way with the first born. There are advantages to being the oldest; but there's also a burden.

Linda went to Weston High School. During the summer, as with all my kids, she got a job. She worked at a nursing home that I owned. She would read books to the elderly residents and talk with them. It was good for them and it was good for Linda. All children should get real-world experience when they are growing up. It grooms them to become a good person.

After high school, Linda went to Westbrook College. And then she came to work for my company.

Linda is a very caring, lovable and passionate person and she loves people. Because she is that type of person, she got herself in trouble with me.

When she went on a date, her curfew was to return home by 11:00 P.M. Many times she came home a little bit late, and I was always at the front door to welcome her in. She didn't see it that way. Another time, she went shopping with a friend and again she came home late; she was punished by not being allowed to go out again for many months. But beside these few things, she has a heart of gold. She reminds me of a mother hen. Everyone wants to be with her. She has raised a wonderful family of her own.

She met a great young man, Jack Kacewicz, who was studying to be an orthodontist. They were married and soon began having a family. They have four children and four grandchildren! That's hard for me to believe sometimes. I'm a great-grandfather.

After Linda, came our daughter Debra—who was born one year later to the day, on December 5, 1953. She was a beautiful baby. She was a colicky child, and that was tough with another baby in the house too. But, you get through these things.

Debra was high spirited. She knew her mind and went after what she wanted. She was very artistic. A very good painter. I have her paintings in my office and in my home.

She went to Weston High School. Then she graduated from Boston University, and for graduate school she went to the Massachusetts College of Art.

Debra was the first of our children to move out of the house. She met a great young man, Dean Lynch, who was an attorney in New York. They married and moved to a nice village just outside of New York City to live.

They soon had a baby, a little girl whom they named Madeline. I was so happy, because this was such a beautiful tribute to their baby's Grandmother Madeline.

But then the unthinkable happened.

Debra got sick. She went for a check-up and the diagnosis was brain cancer.

This couldn't be happening again. How could this be happening again?

You immediately think a range of thoughts: It's not fair, it's not right, it's not true. But it was true. Once again, we were a family struck by cancer. Once again, we were a family that had to pull together—that had to do all the things that had to be done—that had to stay strong.

Debra came to live with me, because she was being treated at Dana-Farber in Boston; so it would be so much more convenient for her.

It was terrible, but I was glad to be with her through it all.

My daughter passed away on September 5, 1996. She was 43 years old, and little Madeline was only four.

Debra had done many paintings, which I have; and she also sold many of her works.

So, somewhere out there, people see Debra's vision of the world in paint—hanging on their walls, perhaps not even knowing who she was or what she went through.

I see her paintings every day. I don't need them to remember who she was and what she went through. I don't need them to remember how wonderful she was or how talented she was. I need them because she was my daughter.

Patricia was our third child. She was born on February 26, 1955, and she was named after me. Well, as close as I could get to Pasquale.

She was very different from Linda and Debra. She was more of a home type. She was very close to her mother. Patricia liked doing housework and cooking.

She also went to Weston High and then graduated from Bentley College in 1976. And she came to work for me. What a business mind she had! She loved our work. She really wanted to be my right-hand person. She loved to be involved with all phases of our projects.

She began in the accounting department, but she enjoyed the action out in the world and she started working as an assistant site manager in one of our apartment complexes; and, later, she managed that apartment complex of 350 units. From there she became the general manager of our real-estate department.

Again, Patty was very close to my wife and me. At one point, she wanted to take over her mother's responsibilities in the house when Madeline passed away. But I didn't think that was a good idea, so I insisted that she move to Cabot Estates, which I owned. It's a very nice place. A gated condominium in Jamaica Plain, across from Jamaica Pond, nestled on 23 acres of forested land.

Patty met a man named Paul Flaherty and they were married. Because she was so involved in her job and loved it so much, she took it upon herself to upgrade the complex without my consent. We had lots of arguments over that, because she didn't want to consult with me. But, at the end of the day, we got over it and all went well.

At this time, we had set up an endowment for research at Dana-Farber. They asked me to be on the board, but that wasn't for me. Patricia did it for me. She became very involved; she loved the work. Our endowment today has grown to more than one-and-a-half million dollars.

Sadly, Patty never had children. She never got the chance.

Incredibly—Patty was diagnosed with ovarian cancer—which is what my Madeline died from.

Once again, we fought the good fight and she found support and love from her family. Once again, we did all the things we thought we could do.

And yet—once again—we had to confront death, we had to confront loss. As unimaginable as this was—we had to say goodbye.

Patricia passed away on August 18, 2005.

Susanne, our fourth child and fourth daughter, was born on November 18, 1954. She was a happy little girl. Like her sisters, she went to Weston High School and then graduated from Colby Sawyer.

During her summers while in school, she was my assistant coach for Little League. She arranged all the times of games and practices. She would call all the players and tell them when and where games and practices would be. She would sit with me and keep score and keep track of all the players. She was just wonderful.

We also played lots of tennis. We would jog together. Best of all, we would ski together—and no matter how difficult a trail would be, she would be right behind me. She truly was a good buddy.

After completing her education, she worked for the Waltham Racquet Club, which I owned, and she ran all the activities for young kids.

Back then, I spent some time each winter in Florida. Right after Susanne graduated from Colby Sawyer, she came for a visit and got a job in a children's day-care facility. She loved it and she asked me if she could stay until the end of the session, because she had given her word to the owner.

I said that would be no problem, since I could trust her and also because I respected her loyalty to the center's owner.

So I got on a plane and went home and Susanne stayed behind to work.

Back home, I'd call Susanne every evening. We had gotten very close in Florida. We went jogging together all the time and we played a lot of tennis. So, I enjoyed talking with her at night.

One night she said, "Dad, I don't feel good."

She said she felt dehydrated.

I told her to see a doctor.

She went to see a doctor down there; they told her to drink more water. But she wasn't feeling any better.

Each night when we spoke, she said she just didn't feel good.

I said, "Susanne, please get on the next plane and come home."

I met her at the airport. She didn't look good at all. We went straight to Newton-Wellesley Hospital.

After many tests, they told us that she had been diagnosed with lung cancer—and that the tumor was inoperable.

She never smoked. No one in the family smoked.

How—how could this be happening? Now it seems odd to even be saying that. Four times. My wife. My daughters.

Together, we went through hospital stays and long treatments.

Together, we huddled and pleaded and hoped and prayed.

Helpless, we saw the fight slip away.

We saw the light flicker and softly go out.

Susanne passed away on June 1, 1973.

She was twenty-one years old. It wasn't a great many years—in terms of length. But it was a great many years in terms of the life she led—and in terms of my heart.

We set up a fund for her—the Madeline-Susanne Franchi Foundation. We called it "Fund for Life." We ran all kinds of activities. We raised lots of money for cancer research.

It wasn't too long after Susanne was born, that our first son, Louie, was born, on March 10, 1964.

We had moved to Weston by then. But, I was working at Cape Canaveral at the time and my sister called and said, "You finally have a boy! Come right home!"

I moved quickly and got home in time to take Madeline and the baby home from the hospital.

I wanted to name him Louis, after my father Luigi.

Madeline said she wanted to name him Steven—and we could have Louis for a middle name.

"But I like Louis for a first name," I said.

"Please make me happy," Madeline said.

So I agreed.x

When time for the Christening came, we were having a big party and Madeline, as was the Italian custom, stayed home to get things ready.

I went to the church and when the priest said, "What do you name this child?" I heard myself saying, "Louis Steven Franchi."

Mind you, we had over fifty people back at the house celebrating the Christening of our first son; the house was all decorated; everyone was expecting me to bring home a boy named Steven.

Uh, oh.

So I got home and I said to Madeline, "Honey, sorry. But I had to name our baby Louis instead of Steven."

She understood. After a few evil eyes.

We had a good party and all ended well.

Louie is a really good athlete. He went to the Rivers School in Weston for High School, where he was a great football player and wrestler. He was also really good at golf, tennis and skiing.

During his summers, he worked for me as an assistant carpenter, a laborer, working on homes we were building.

He went to the University of Rhode Island—but after a couple of years I realized he was mostly partying, so I sent him to the Wentworth Institute in Boston, where he graduated with a technical degree.

As I said, Louie was really a good kid, but he wanted to experience many things and he loved parties. Along with that, I was concerned about some of his friends. They liked beer. Lots of beer. So when he asked me to let him throw parties at our house, I said yes—but with the understanding that he invite a limited number of friends. Of course, before I realized it, there were tons and tons of kids at our house! But I made sure that no one was hurt and I had my girls be chaperons with me.

At that time, I had a restaurant with a bar in my Waltham Tennis Club. One day, I sent Louie to clean the restaurant. I happened to stop by and saw Louie and a couple of buddies at the bar having a beer. They were all under-age. I really got upset and sent Louie home to wait for me by the pool. It was August, a hot, hot day, and I took a case of beer with me to the pool. I made Louie sit in a chair and I explained to him that what he had done was wrong and that I could have lost my liquor license. I took each bottle of beer, one after the other, and poured each one over his head. When I was done, I said that I hoped this had taught him a lesson about responsibility. We had a few of these kinds of get togethers from time to time, but, thank God, it all has worked out well. Now he is married and has four beautiful children and is a very responsible person.

Let me say right here that I know parents today will think I'm too harsh—maybe too old-school. But, you have to make a point sometimes. And you have to be firm. Children—even older children—want to know where they stand. My kids always knew where they stood. So I don't dwell on things. I did what I had to do to make sure my children were responsible for their actions.

As for Louie, well, he met the woman he would marry at U.R.I.—Deirdre Hayes. I was so pleased that he liked such a very wonderful young lady, and I was very happy when they were married several years later.

Louie came to work for me. He was in charge of a big time-share project in North Conway, New Hampshire. He built the time-share units and oversaw the time-share operation, which ended up being very challenging and, yet, very successful as well. Louie also ran a tennis club we owned there.

I'll always remember one thing that happened with Louie and me —as well as with my son Michael—that shows you what families are about. It was a weekend at Christmas, when we were up at Wildcat trying to get a big remodeling project done for Christmas Day. Louie, Michael and I were painting the lodge.

It was late on Christmas Eve and we stayed up mostly all night painting the main hall of the lodge. We didn't see Santa, but we finished in time for our guests to enjoy the new room on Christmas morning.

I liked that. I liked that we pitched in. We were a family. We worked together.

Well, a few years after that, Louie and Deirdre had a little girl, who they named Jessica. In fact, there's a street we built in the development of time-share units that we called Jessica Way after her.

When I visited them in New Hampshire, I babysat for them and it came time when the baby needed to have her diaper changed. I managed to do it, since I did have experience with my six children. But it had been a while! Anyway, Jessica and I have always been quite close.

Eventually, Louie and family moved back to Boston. They had three more children. Louie still works for me—he is our vice-president.

Our sixth child was Michael, who was born on October 22, 1966. We thought we would stop after having five kids, but sometimes you get a very nice surprise.

Once again my sister called and said, "Your Madeline has just given birth to your second son."

This was when I was in Tunisia building the University of Tunis. I took off as soon as I could to get home. At the hospital, nurses were betting that I wouldn't get there in time to check my wife out.

They would have lost that bet. It was close, but I made it.

I loved having little Michael. Now there were two brothers—two boys—close in age who could play together growing up.

Michael followed his brother at the Rivers School. He was a good student and a very good athlete. He was a great baseball and football player. I remember when the football coach told me that Michael had great hands, that he was really good at catching passes. He was also a really great tennis player. He and I played a lot. In fact, that prompted me to build a tennis court at home. That way, I could enjoy playing while also being able to keep an eye on the kids! Which worked, because one day we were playing—the court is about 100 yards from the house—and I knew Patty was inside baking brownies. I could smell something burning. I told Michael to run inside and tell his sister that the brownies were burning. They were.

"How in the world did you know?" Patty asked me.

The only answer is that parents know.

After high school, Michael went to Boston College, where he did well in school and was captain of the tennis team.

After graduation from college, he decided to try professional tennis. He was assigned to a pro circuit that played in Europe—Spain, Italy, France—as well as in South America. He was ranked 1200th in the world.

After a few years traveling all over the world, he came home and said, "Dad, I'm done with tennis."

So—a little ironically—I put him in the assistant-manager position at the tennis club that I owned in Waltham. He eventually became manager of the club and excelled at the job. He renamed the club the Waltham Athletic Club, giving it a wider appeal, and that's how it is known today.

After that, well, things took a turn.

When Patty died, Michael was affected very seriously. He was very close to her. He really looked up to her and admired her and loved her. Her death pushed him over the edge. He became very depressed and isolated. He stopped working. He still manages to come to dinner some Sundays. I hope that with time he'll reclaim his life.

Loss is hard. So very hard. To have four members of our family taken by cancer was almost more than all of us could endure.

Linda, Louie, Michael and I have no choice but to endure.

We have to.

For each other.

And for the memory of Madeline, Debra, Patricia and Susanne.

Of course, you always want to help those who helped you—and you want to help, if you can, other families who are going through similar ordeals.

I have nothing but admiration for Newton-Wellesley Hospital—the doctors and nurses and the entire staff. They were simply wonderful to my entire family.

I served on the hospital board for a while—like I said, hoping to help. And I donated a new lobby area where patients check in, the Madeline Franchi Lobby. Later, I donated a new oncology suite, the Susanne Franchi Oncology Suite.

Beyond medical care, I've always liked to do things for families—because the family is the backbone of any country.

I was very happy to help with the Boys & Girls Club of Newton. I served as a director, vice-president and president; and I helped raise money for a number of activities.

PAT FRANCHI

I have a special place in my heart for the Home for Little Wanderers in Walpole. They have been doing great work for over 200 years—providing a wide range of services to more than 7,000 children and young adults each year. I donated the Pat Franchi and Family Gymnasium which provides a lot of services and good fun for the boys and girls. They were nice enough to give me their Service Award in 2011. I also set it up so that my monthly Social Security check is given to the Home for Little Wanderers. I've been doing that for 20 years and hope to do it for many, many more years.

I also like to help Boys Town—because they do such great work. And I am happy to give to the American Cancer Society and as many other charities as I can.

On the business side of life, I've served as a member of the Board of Directors for the Guaranteed First National Bank in Waltham, Massachusetts.

I remember an odd little story that shows how sometimes you have to trust your instinct. There was a young man I knew—hardly knew at the time—named John Cannistraro. John came to see me for a loan so that he could start his own plumbing and heating company. He had tried to get a loan from a bank, and also from his relatives, without being successful. So he finally came to me and requested a loan of $5,000. I believed in him because he was so sincere. I had faith in him. I not only gave him the money, but I also gave him his first job on a nursing home that I was building.

John paid the loan back, of course, and today the company he started has become one of the most successful plumbing and heating companies in the Boston area, and his family still runs the business. John and I remain friends to this day.

Whether it's helping someone you know, or perfect strangers, or the community in which you live—I think it's important for all of us to try and do what we can to help another person to succeed.

Because, as simple as this may sound, we're all in this together.

CHAPTER EIGHTEEN
Christmas Carols

Let me tell you a Christmas story that happened back in the old days, when I was full of energy and full of the Christmas spirit. These were the days when we worked hard and played hard —all in good fun.

It was late afternoon around 6:30 P.M. on the day before Christmas Eve. It was snowing outside my office, and, with all the Christmas spirit that was built into me and with everything going so well in my life and with my business, I was really a happy person.

So, all of a sudden, it came to me that I should call a few buddies and go out singing Christmas carols to my friends. I proceeded to do just that. I called my wife Madeline and told her what I planned to do. She said to go ahead and have fun.

I immediately called my very best friend, Danny Antonelli, who was also in the construction business—we also played lots of golf together and we took many vacations together with our wives. He answered the phone and I asked what his plans were that evening. He replied that he and his wife were going to a dinner party with a few friends. I told him that he had to get to my office quickly, because I needed to discuss a very important issue with him.

I had to trick him, otherwise I knew he wouldn't have come to my office. He said he would come, but he added that he couldn't stay too long because he and his wife had those dinner plans. I promised him it wouldn't take too long.

In the meantime, I called another friend, Tony Marini, who had a very good voice and played the accordion. I also called another friend, John DeFillippo, who played the clarinet.

When Danny arrived and found out what my plans were, he was concerned that he would not be able to get back in time to take his wife to the dinner party. I promised him that he'd make it.

So we set out on our trip in my car. Our first stop was Joe Farina's house and our second stop was Louis Racine's house—who were both very good friends of mine as well.

We got out and began to sing carols at Joe's front door. Of course, he opened the door to us and we walked into his kitchen and had a Christmas toast.

We left—with Joe joining our company!

Then we went to Louis Racine's house and then my brother Jerry's house and did the same thing.

On and on it went. We were having such a good time and we didn't realize how late it was. Meanwhile, Danny's wife kept calling my poor wife and was giving her a hard time because I had taken Danny away.

Of course my Madeline didn't know where we were. There were no cell phones back then—thank God!

At almost every house where we stopped, we picked up another person. We got to the point where we had at least fifteen to twenty people in our group! This caroling caravan went on until after midnight. We finally stopped at Michael Pirolli's home in Watertown at about 12:30 A.M. We sang, and we drank another toast.

Then Michael and his wife graciously made us all breakfast—and that became a tradition for the next three years.

After eating, any thought of quitting disappeared. So we hit the road again.

We stopped in at my younger brother Tony and his wife Connie's house in Newton at about 3:00 A.M. His door was unlocked so we went in and went right to their bedroom!

I pulled the covers and sheets off of the bed—I really did that. They were left wearing whatever they had on and we sang our Christmas carols and had our toast and moved on to Waltham.

We stopped at Lino Nardone's house. Again the door was unlocked and we went to his bedroom and sang "Jingle Bells."

We then drove to Belmont, to my very good friend Jim Duff's house—who was having a party and his guests were getting ready to leave. When they saw us, singing our way into the house, they went back inside too!

But Jim Duff didn't know who I was because I was dressed in a Santa Claus suit. Oh, that's right, I forgot to mention that somewhere along the route I acquired a Santa suit.

Anyway, I took off my beard and he recognized me and we joined the party.

At last, it was time to go home.

On the way, we saw people going into the six o'clock Mass.

Danny was really concerned that he was in deep trouble with his wife—but he said he had had a good time so it would be worth it.

I remember that all night long we had been traipsing into people's homes, unannounced and uninvited, tracking in wet snow and slush and messing up everyone's floors, but each and every one enjoyed our surprise.

Maybe it was just a simpler time.

Maybe people had more Christmas spirit back then.

I don't know. But I do know that people loved it when we showed up. Unannounced. Wet and messy. Singing!

In fact, we did this for several more years.

But Danny never came again.

CHAPTER NINETEEN
New and Old Chapters

Several years after Madeline passed away, I met a young lady. Fran Towle. We met playing golf at the Charles River Country Club.

It took me many months before I could get up the nerve to ask her out. But I did and we've become very close.

Fran never married and doesn't have children of her own, but she is now part of our family and is very close to the kids—she's always helped me keep tabs on them.

We call Fran the birthday-cake maker. She bakes the best birthday cakes for all the children. They put their requests in to her at Christmas time—and she knows all about the actual type of cake they prefer and she makes it for them at their birthdays. Fran knows all of my kids' birthdays—which even I have a hard time remembering.

She's very intelligent, a very caring person, and a good arguer—which galls me because she tries to beat the hell out of me in golf and she tries to win every argument we have over scores and shots and penalties. It's all healthy discussions—lively give-and-take.

We all carry sadness. Every person in the world. Mostly, it doesn't show.

That's because no one ever knows what happens at night when you're all alone or when you're driving or when you're sitting by yourself in a coffee shop.

Fran helps me. She helps the kids in many ways. We are very lucky to have Fran in our lives.

BUILDING MY LIFE

What also helps a lot, of course, is keeping busy. Work helps me from thinking about the past all the time. And with all the new projects ahead of me, I hope that the Good Lord will grant me an extension of my life so that I can see the fruits of what I have planned.

I must do that for my children—I must put sadness aside as much as I can and look forward to tomorrow.

I have nine grandchildren and four great-grandchildren.

I've said over and over again that family is so very important. That's why I used to insist that we all go away for one family trip a year for ten days.

We've had many ski trips, and trips to Florida—as well as the Grand Canyon and a real cattle drive!

One favorite spot was the Basin Harbor club in Vermont. We'd get there, park the cars, and have fun. We'd have our own golf and tennis tournaments. And we'd talk it all over each night at dinner together.

It seems that all good things come to an end.

We don't go on our trips any more. As time goes by, children get older and have different commitments or obligations. Therefore, it gets very difficult to put together a big trip. So we've had to stop. I still miss it very much.

But, of course, we still get together on Thanksgiving—always at my house.

In fact, the one condition I had before I gave my blessing on any of my children's marriages was that they must have Thanksgiving at my house.

It's wonderful. I bake a thirty-pound turkey with all the fixings.

The stuffing, however, is controversial.

I use my mother's recipe, and have never told anyone what the ingredients are. They always question what's in it and I never tell them.

And they never eat it!

Fran makes her own stuffing. She gets the front end of the bird to stuff and I get the other. They like hers better than mine. But mine is the one that gives the meal its aroma.

The other thing I'm good at is meatballs. I use bread crumbs instead of chunks of bread. Lots of garlic, parsley, cheese, eggs and salt. And I cook them in the sauce; I don't fry them first. Italians are pretty much divided on this very important issue of life. I think my way is the best way. And I get no complaints.

I still cook every Sunday. I have the entire family join in—those who can make it—and we have dinner together. I really enjoy that. Everyone sitting around the table. Talking. Eating. Laughing.

It's a lot of work, but well worth it.

It gives everyone a chance—especially the young children—to be together. I'm tired every Sunday night, but I wouldn't trade it for anything.

Family. Food. Fun.

Nothing takes away the sadness, but we find ways to endure.

CHAPTER TWENTY
Back to the Land

It takes a special person who has great vision to purchase a piece of land and be able to visualize what you could create on this space. Anybody can buy a piece of land. But the most important thing is how you develop it—what kind of structure you are going to design and then build and what return you will get after making the investment.

Owning a piece of land is better than owning gold. Land will never go away. Gold may lose its value. But land never loses its value. It's there for you to take and make it happy and pleased. I look at a piece of land like having a new baby. What type of baby should I raise for this property? And how will I be rewarded in the future? It really is like raising a child. If you do a good job raising your child, you will be very proud. It's the same thing with land. You pick up a piece of land and design a building on it that will improve the area and it will reward you with a good financial return.

Key to creating a good development is to have the vision of location, location, location! Then you have to ask yourself, what is your vision for? How will you develop this unique piece of land— what will you do that will make you proud when you're done?

So, let me tell you about some of the visions I've had and what they became.

One of my very first ventures was Albemarle Gardens, in Newtonville. This site was a dump at one time. But again—location, location, location. I purchased the site and designed a garden type of apartment complex, with one- and two-bedroom units. I can't tell you how much I enjoyed that. I was very happy and proud that I had taken a piece of land that was used as a city dump and had brought it to life again.

The next site was Town Estates. This was a large piece of land in Melrose, Massachusetts, that had been purchased by another developer —but no one had the courage to build on it because the land had lots of "peat." Again, vision comes to play. I liked the location but I also realized I had a soil problem. I thought about it for a few days and I saw that it would cost a little bit more than what the original buyer paid, but I was confident that I could make up the additional cost and more in the long run. So I bought the land and I constructed a 265-unit apartment complex that has many amenities, such as tennis courts and a swimming pool. It's been very successful—and, again, I felt the pride of taking a piece of land that nobody dared to develop and made it something successful.

A really interesting project was Bass Point, a 128-unit residence in Nahant, Massachusetts. It's located on a peninsula with water on both sides. I bought the land and was getting ready to start, when we hit a zoning issue. The town wanted a marina and a hotel. I didn't want to build a marina or a hotel.

I owned the land and thought a marina was not the best use of the land—so I fought the town on this issue. We reached a compromise. Finally, after meetings and discussions and more and more meetings, they said I could build the apartment complex but that it had to *look* like a boat motel type of building and could only have one-bedroom units.

I took out my vision cap and I could see that the plan was possible. So I went ahead.

We constructed Bass Point and rented the 128 units. All went well. The town was happy and I was happy. That was until an un-named hurricane came along and caused a lot of very serious damage to the complex. Most of the roof and siding was damaged. Gone with the wind! Eleven units were completely destroyed—swept into the Atlantic Ocean. But I went ahead and rebuilt the eleven units and repaired all the other damage. Finally I was able to obtain permission to extend a concrete wall along the Atlantic Ocean side—which, to date, has worked perfectly. Again, the complex is doing fine and I'm proud of the vision that got it going in the first place. Oh, the name. I called it Bass Point because back in the old days this was a favorite spot for Native Americans to fish for bass.

After that came Kendall Crossing. This apartment complex consisted of 330 garden-type units located in a very nice spot in Natick, Massachusetts. I didn't get a chance to use any vision on this one because I took over this project during the construction phase. The original developer got in trouble with the bank and therefore we made an agreement that I would take over the completion of the site, and I released the original developer of all financial obligations. Well, that part did take some vision, I guess, and I'm glad to say that today this complex is doing just fine.

Then came Babcock Tower in Boston. It's a 24-story building with 230 apartments, plus it has 230 underground parking spaces. There's also some commercial space on the ground floor. Again, this building is doing very well and again I am very proud of the results.

I went farther north, and built the Crown Ridge Resort in North Conway, New Hampshire. These were ski chalets that I put up next to Mt. Cranmore. I did this while I was building in the Boston area and Franchi Construction was also working on major construction projects for other owners. Well, the old vision cap didn't work too well on the ski chalets, so I had to shift gears to re-coup my investment on the project.

I decided to turn the units into timeshares. Oh, boy, what an experience that was! Anyway, after several years we've sold out the whole complex. It was a pain—but it turned out to be successful. I give credit to my son Louie who was completely responsible for seeing the project through all of the ups and downs. You may think that automobile sales people are a little bit flaky, but they're nothing compared to time-share sales people—they can convince you that the sun is shining while it's pouring rain outside. We had a very hard time keeping those sales people on track—making sure they were truthful and honest with our customers. It was hard to control them! But, in the end it all worked out fine. Another great experience.

In Bartlett, New Hampshire, we bought a site on the side of a mountain and created a housing development. The views from the homes are unbelievable. The site is completed and all the homeowners are very happy.

We also own a very large parcel of land that abuts Cranmore Mountain that I will develop one day. But, my vision cap tells me to wait a couple more years. The people who will eventually live there will be able to ski out of their homes directly onto the slopes!

Location, location, location.

Another project was Brimstone Estates, consisting of about 45 acres located on the side of Nobscot Mountain in Framingham, Massachusetts. I bought this land back in 1984 and my vision told me not to start development until recently. Today, it is the only gated community in Framingham. We've completed two homes in the million-dollar range and we'll start the third home soon. I'm sure this project will be very successful.

I bought the site known as the Marsh, in South Dartmouth, Massachusetts, because it's right on the bay. Location! There's also a 9-hole golf course and lots of places of historic interest in the area. Anyway, my son Louie and I built a few houses on the site which have been very well received by owners. I'm satisfied this will continue to be a very nice development and it will grow.

Next door, in North Dartmouth, we've completed a subdivision known as Gendreau Estates; and we hope to start construction on a number of houses very soon.

Sometimes, a bit of chance is involved. For instance, in the early 1990s, my son Louie and I had some business with the Riverside condo project in Haverhill, Massachusetts. A friend suggested that I take a look at a building he owned at 72 Washington Street. So Louie and I looked at the building and I put on the old vision cap and I liked the location. It was right on the main street in downtown and it backed up to the Merrimack River. There were beautiful architectural design elements on the exterior of the building. On the ride home, I discussed it with Louie and we decided to buy it. Our plan was to put in parking under the ground floor, retail space on the first floor and apartments on the other floors. So while the architect was working on drawings, I got a demolition permit from the city and I hired a contractor to begin the excavation job for the parking garage. Unfortunately, while this work was going on, there was a fire one weekend and the entire building was so badly damaged that we had to tear it all down. Since then we have replaced it with a new 54-unit complex called Riverside Place. There are 54 two-bedroom units with underground parking. Half the units overlook the Mystic River and the others face Washington Street.

Now, a little history of our commercial sites.

I built my first office for Franchi Construction on Webster Street in West Newton.

But we soon outgrew that space. So I bought the building at 425 Watertown Street, because it was the original office that the Farina Brothers operated, and this is where my father worked for them for many years until he retired at close to 70 years old. My brother and I worked for the Farina Brothers too. So there was a little bit of history tied up in the building as well. My company worked there until I phased out the company—and at that time I remodeled the space for office use and I also built warehouse space in the rear of the building. The entire complex is rented today and doing very well.

My next venture was to build an office building at 182 West Central Street, in Natick, Massachusetts; it houses a number of tenants and it's also the headquarters of my company, Franchi Management. Getting this building started wasn't too easy though. The land was a mountain of ledge—no one wanted it, it would be too expensive to build on. So I bought it at a very good price—and started getting all the ledge out, using large vibrating digging machines. And, I found a contractor who would haul the ledge away for free, because he could sell it to another company that used it as an aggregate for making concrete and asphalt. This is another example of how you have to have a vision about how you can get things done at a reasonable cost.

Meanwhile, another opportunity was pointed out to me—a very large warehouse at 25 Kenwood Drive in Franklin, Massachusetts. The structure was being taken over by the bank, so I put on the vision cap and I decided to purchase the site from the bank. We finished the remaining work and we have rented the entire space of 85,000 square feet.

While I was negotiating with the bank for this property, they brought to my attention that they had another large lot of land that they had to take back from the same developer.

So I bought that one too! We built a very nice warehouse with 121,000 square feet. It also is fully rented and doing very well. I must say that I was pleased with how it all turned out.

After that, I purchased Natick Crossing, at 251 West Central Street—which consists of approximately 56,500 square feet of retail and office space on its two floors. I bought it because our office is very close to it and that makes it easy to manage and oversee. It's fully rented and doing very well.

Next in Natick, I bought 220 North Main Street, which consists of three office buildings with a large parcel of undeveloped land in the rear; I'd like to convince the town to rezone that land so I can build more office space. Like the others, this is all fully rented and doing well.

Recently, we purchased another building at 212 North Main Street in Natick. So, you see, we now own a very large frontage on

Route 27 and very close to Route 9. Our vision is to one day tear down this building and create a beautiful new office and retail space.

A few years ago, I purchased an office building on Speen Street in neighboring Framingham; it's four stories high with 33,000 square feet of rental space. I really like its location, since it is very close to the entrance to the Mass Pike and other main routes.

Then there's Cochituate Place in Natick, the largest office building in our portfolio—more than 110,000 square feet, with all the amenities —a cafeteria, a gym and so on. It's our flagship. It's a Type-A office building, with a great location near all major routes; it has top-of-the line furnishings and appointments, all done by a very good interior-design firm.

I've found over the years that office space is very much easier to manage than housing space.

Now let me tell you about one very innovative project—I led the way in this area—which was the Waltham Racquet Club. I used to play a lot of golf. But after Madeline passed away, I realized that golf took a great deal of time and kept me away from the children. So I switched to tennis, and I joined the Boston Athletic Club.

But I could never get enough court time. One of my tennis partners suggested that we build our own tennis club. He had the land and I would be the builder. So we went in on it together—but I made sure that I owned 51 percent of the project, as I provided financing, design and construction.

What I did differently was that I built the first racquet club that also had a swimming pool—as well as racquetball courts and a very fine restaurant. After my success, other clubs followed suit.

But the venture had a sour ending. My partner and I didn't see eye-to-eye on anything. One day he said, "It's time one of us has to go."

So I bought him out. I could have kicked him out since I owned 51 percent, but I didn't.

Still—my advice is never go into a partnership unless you have the controlling interest.

What next?

Well, recently, I've gone south and started projects in Florida.

I didn't really "go" south—I've been there for quite a while, but in a different capacity.

Let me explain.

I have owned a condominium at the Sundial Resort in Sanibel Island for many years. But I'm not a beach person, nor do I pick up shells. I like to play golf or tennis and to jog along the beach. I do enjoy the beach, but I can't just sit under an umbrella gazing at the ocean.

But also I can't play golf every day, so, not to get bored, I started looking at real estate. I couldn't help myself! I saw this one parcel that contained a partially completed home-site subdivision called Meadows Edge. It had 56 lots, all subdivided with the roads already in. So I bought it!

My vision said, "Do it, Pat." So I did it.

Across the street, there was another parcel of 85 house lots called Heron Glade and my trusty vision said to buy it because it would be great in a few years.

Then a parcel of land came up for sale right at the end of my street which was zoned for commercial use—it's called Savannah Lakes.

"Pat," my vision said, "buy this parcel and you will have control of the entire intersection."

Plus it was zoned for business which made it great to build a shopping center on this section of land. I hope the Good Lord will give me time to complete this new vision.

There's another project that I really have liked working on called the Cypress Lake Condominium Complex. It's on Winkler Road in Fort Myers. I joined a golf club in Fort Myers and while I was playing golf I saw a piece of land that abutted the golf course. It had a very good location. I visualized a great spot for an apartment complex. So I bought it! I teamed up with a very nice local developer and we started building housing units.

However, they were costing us much more than what we could sell them for, so the complex was not very successful financially. But it's a very attractive complex that I'm proud of. We lost money, but I'm still pleased with the final result.

Then there came a day when a real estate broker called to my attention a 300-unit condominium project that was started by another developer which, unfortunately for the developer, had been lost to the bank during the recession. So I went ahead and bought it.

I named this site Casa Di Fiore—House of Flowers—which consists of really beautiful condominiums in Cape Coral. It's a gated community with gorgeous units that have all the amenities. All of them.

And, again—location, location, location.

Casa Di Fiore is in a great location, near a shopping center, restaurants, main highways and the city.

I'm very pleased with the sales so far and I'm sure the complex will be very successful.

Years before, a similar thing happened back in Massachusetts with the Dedham Mall. The owner ran out of money and I came in to finish the project. It wasn't easy, though—there were a number of arguments—but we finally worked things out.

What I'm telling you is that you can seize certain opportunities that present themselves—but you have to be very careful who you do business with and you have to have control of the project. Otherwise it just isn't worth doing.

While all of this is going on, my children tell me to play more golf—but I love what I'm doing and it gives me a lot of satisfaction. Besides, the more golf I play, the more land I see and then I want to buy it!

With all of this work, with all of this buying and building and selling, what it came down to was that I could see what the land could bring to you, if you can visualize the type of development you propose. Each site is different from the one you just completed.

So it's really important that you do your homework before you dig a hole in the ground.

Which, I guess, is one reason why people come to me for advice.

Way back, when I was a general contractor, I was asked to be on the board of the AGC—the Associated General Contractors of America. I got involved in union issues, labor disputes, wage negotiations and on and on.

Members of the AGC had to sign an agreement that we would hire only union employees. At the same time, I could see lots of other work being done by non-union contractors. I brought this matter up to the board at one of our meetings.

I asked, "Why can't we do both?"

Everyone thought I was crazy.

But my idea was to set up one company for union work and a second company for non-union work. In this way, I could hire a lot more people for jobs—often it was the same people who worked in my union projects—and I could switch them to work on non-union jobs and could pay them wages and benefits according to the rules governing union jobs.

After many discussions with the union and members of the AGC, everyone finally saw the light and gave me the go ahead.

I set up Eastern Builders, a non-union company that would work only on non-union jobs. We use an awful lot of union workers, people who need the work, and pay them union wages and benefits.

It worked well for everyone. More people worked. The unions weren't hurt. Workers were paid well either way.

I was the guinea pig. Once the other contractors saw that my vision was working, they also jumped on the band wagon. The whole concept got the nickname of "Double Breast." And it worked.

My non-union company has been very successful and, in fact, it's still operating.

You need to have a vision if you want to be successful.

BUILDING MY LIFE

CHAPTER TWENTY-ONE
Money

Recently, I've thought a lot about money.

I've done very well, for a young man starting a company with $300 mustering-out pay from the U.S. Marine Corps. And that has benefited me and my family. Because of the company I've built—because of all the hard work—my children are millionaires in their own right.

Which I thought was a wonderful thing that I did for my family. I came to this country from Italy when I was twelve years old and had nothing. I worked at Peter Volante Farm for wages of seven-and-a-half cents an hour. And today, my children never have to work if they don't want to. We're not fabulously rich, but we're in a very, very comfortable position.

None of my children ever had to knock on other people's doors trying to get any type of jobs. My children have had all of their education paid for—all paid in full. And more and more beyond that.

Lately, however, I feel as though I've been stabbed in the heart.

A couple of things have happened that have shown me that even your own family—even your own children—when confronted with a lot of money—can put money above honor. I won't go into the details here. These are private matters. And, I know that the right things will be done in time.

Maybe there's just something about money. Maybe money has the power to create disrespect, lying, manipulation—and betrayal.

I hate feeling this way. And I know I'll get over it. And I know all will be all right once again. Someday.

I see many close friends and families not speaking to each other over money. Sometimes, they've gotten involved in court cases because they have disputed an inheritance. Or I've seen people try to find a way out of loans which were made in good faith with a big heart—but, when the time arrived to pay back one of these good-faith loans, the recipient found reasons not to pay it back, and there goes a friend or family member.

I'm a strong believer that you should be able to help a friend or a family member but you should do it properly with good legal documents and proof of how a loan is going to be paid back, otherwise you might as well consider it a gift from the start. So don't allow your heart to control your decision. George Washington is good to have but you need to use him properly.

But if someone ever says to me that if they had more money then they'd be happy, I'll answer that money is a two-way street. It can take you to happiness, or, without any warning, it can take you to sorrow.

Money to me is not how much you have—or not something to use to show off. But it's a tool that I use in business, instead of using picks and shovels.

I use money to bargain for leverage on a business deal. It makes a big difference if you have the cash readily available to make the deal, instead of hoping to get a loan. A seller always prefers dealing with a person who has cash, instead of a person making an offer that is subject to getting a loan.

I have always been a hard-bargaining person, but I have never reneged on any deal. Once I give my word, I honor it no matter what.

There's nothing wrong with being frugal, but it is wrong if you are dishonest or a fake.

You should treat others just like you want to be treated.

Being honest and truthful is something that nobody can take away from you.

You should always remember to put yourself in the other person's shoes, and ask yourself: Is this honest? Is this fair and just? Is this the right thing to do?

How would I feel if I were the person being betrayed or taken advantage of?

My mother always said, If you bite someone it will come back to bite you.

So, I say: Be honest and loyal to your fellow man and in return you will also be respected.

This is especially true when it comes to family.

To take advantage of someone in your own family is betrayal, pure and simple. You expect your own family members to treat you with fairness—with more than fairness. I just can't imagine why anyone would ever want to take advantage of someone in their own family.

And as I get older—I feel more and more strongly about this.

Family should be love.

Never betrayal.

CHAPTER TWENTY-TWO
Bocce—and Those Other Sports

From a very young age, I always liked sports. When I was in school in Italy, we played soccer. When I came to America, I wanted to play baseball, football and hockey. Soccer was not popular in America back then.

But I couldn't tell my folks that I wanted to play, because they thought I could get hurt. They also thought that my time would be better spent working around the house or doing assigned chores.

So I had to play without anyone knowing.

I had a list of chores to do every day after school. But I'd sneak out to play sports—baseball and football and so on.

In order for me to be able to play, I would make deals with my little brother and sister to do my work, so that I wouldn't get scolded at the evening dinner.

I got away with it! I played sports all the time, and my parents never knew it.

Of course, they never saw me play. They never went to a game. Because they didn't know I was playing.

For hockey, I'd hide my skates and my equipment—and then sneak it all out of the house and go to the local pond. On one late afternoon while I was skating on the pond, I saw a young boy who had fallen in the water. I skated to him and I pulled him out of the water. I believe it was reported in the newspaper. But I don't know what happened to the article.

For baseball, I played a lot of pick-up games, and I'd sneak out whenever I could and run to the field and play and then sneak back home.

I still have scars from getting hurt, but I never showed them to my parents because I probably would have gotten more punishment.

But mostly I have great memories from participating in these sports, and I'm sorry that I wasn't able to do more.

Then there was bocce.

Bocce is the Italian game where two teams take turns throwing—more like bowling—heavy wooden balls at a target ball to score points. There's a lot of strategy involved. And, it being an Italian game, there's also a lot of screaming and arguing and good wine and bad cigars.

I loved playing bocce with my father. It was great fun to do it together. We belonged to a society, and many members played bocce. We played at a playground on Sunday afternoons. My father and I would play, and then we'd go home to have dinner. After I married Madeline, I played a lot with my father-in-law as well.

Eventually, I became president of the society—the Atina San Marco Society, which was named after the church of Saint Marco in the small Italian town of Atina near my hometown of Gallinaro. The society was in Newton and there wasn't much to it. There was only a little cubbyhole of a building, but I convinced every member to let me convert it to a small clubhouse. It was a place to hang out, and the men would play cards and read papers and talk.

I even set up an Italian school, where we'd hired a teacher to explain Italian culture to our children, but, unfortunately, it only lasted a short period of time. The kids had other things to do and, further, the parents didn't push their children to attend. So they stopped coming and we finally closed the school.

Getting back to bocce, the little target ball is called the boccino, and whoever got to throw it could influence the game. For instance, I'd throw it really far, which gave us younger players an advantage. The old guys didn't like that! They would yell and scream, but as long as I was the captain of my team I could do what I pleased. I was a bad, bad man.

Then comes golf.

When I was dating Madeline, we'd be driving by different country clubs and I would say to Madeline, "Can you believe those crazy people out there? They hit a little white ball, then they chase it and hit it again. Absolutely no brains!"

But then one day a good friend of mine asked me to go out and hit a few balls at the driving range.

Well, that wasn't so bad.

Then he persisted that I go out with him and play a round of golf.

So, here we go. I had to get up at 5:00 A.M., so that I could get home at a decent time.

Well, I got the bug. I played a lot after that. We played at the public golf course for several years, but it would take us something like six hours to play a round of golf, which Madeline and I weren't too happy about. So I decided to join a country club. I looked around and chose Oakley Country Club in Watertown, Massachusetts, which was close to my office.

It wasn't long before I became very active in the club, and I also became a pretty good golfer. I had a handicap of eight, which is not the best, but not bad either. I won my share of tournaments. I would bring home a silver cup or a silver tray and my wife would say, "Here's another piece of silver that I have to clean."

Many times she would use them as flower pots.

In the meantime, I introduced a bocce game at the club, which became really popular. And, as per usual, after many arguments during a game we'd go into the club and have a nice dinner. It was lots of fun.

At that time, I was chosen to obtain bids to construct the irrigation system for the entire eighteen-hole course. Which I did. They then requested that I supervise the installation, and I agreed. I'm happy to say that all the members were very satisfied with the outcome.

Then, the clubhouse burned down! It happened during the night and it was really destroyed. I was asked once again to take charge, and to hire an architect and oversee the rebuilding of the clubhouse. Which I did.

I would do anything else that needed to be done. I was frequently asked, and I was always happy to help.

Three other projects were the swimming pool, tennis courts and pro shop.

After that, they asked me to be in charge of the Grounds Committee, which I accepted. I set right to work. We had all the sand traps redone, and then we worked on the roughs. I directed the ground crew to let the grass grow much higher than normal. Once your ball went in there, you were in trouble! You'd have a hard time finding the ball—not to mention that that would cost you one stroke as well. Can I tell you that I was not popular! People called them the Franchi Roughs!

The Club President asked that I accept a position on the Board of Directors. I did and soon after I was elected vice president and then president of the club.

At my first meeting as president, I set up the different committees —and I took the leadership myself of the House Committee, since that department lost lots of money each year. The first thing I did was to replace the existing manager. I also hired new cooks. The volume of food that was consumed began to increase, but the atmosphere of the dining area wasn't elegant. The paint was discolored, the carpet was old and raggedy. The furniture was old and the chairs would wobble and squeak.

I took it upon myself to redecorate the entire place. I hired an interior decorator to come up with designs and we started to get bids to do the work and we got bids for new furniture.

But, I knew if I brought this up for approval to the Board, they would not go along with it. So I took the bull by the horns and I went downtown to Watertown Square to the Union National Bank, which was the club bank, and spoke to the bank president.

I said that we needed $250,000 for a project that we were doing at the club.

Believe it or not, he approved the loan with no problem whatsoever.

So I went ahead and remodeled the entire clubhouse, including new paint, new carpeting and all new furniture.

Eventually, of course, people found out what I had done!

I thought I was going to be impeached at the upcoming annual meeting.

As it turned out, it was the shortest annual meeting on record. Hey, I had made money for the club—it turned a profit for the first time in years! After the annual meeting, we officers went into a private room for the meeting of the Board of Directors. As president, I appointed committee chairmen of each department and I requested to be re-appointed for one more year as Chairman of the House Committee. This department had lost money every year before I took it over, and therefore I wanted to be involved on a daily basis to oversee the operation.

One director stood up and objected to me again taking over the House Committee. No reason was given for his objection, so a vote was taken and I lost by one vote.

If I couldn't be House Chairman, then I said I wouldn't be President either—because I didn't want to take blame for the poor operation of the House Committee.

So I resigned. I quit the club. That was the end for me at Oakley Country Club. I never went back.

What I did was move on. What else can one do?

I joined the Charles River Country Club in Newton, where I still play today. Naturally, I got involved there as well.

The club had to rebuild its swimming pool, and I was on the committee.

After many meetings we came up with a plan, hired an architect and put the project out to bid. We got four bids and they were all pretty high. I negotiated with the general contractors and finally had an agreement with one of them. Unfortunately, it didn't go ahead. He backed out.

So, we decided to do it ourselves. I became the general contractor for the club on all its projects—the pool, the tennis courts and the beautiful new pavilion.

I used my company, Eastern Builders, and we went ahead and did all the work on time and under budget. It was all very successful. There are 300 members in the club and I never had one complaint.

Then I was responsible for building the Pavilion—which is really a nice touch to the club. They used to have an old tent structure that was in really bad shape. Originally, they wanted to take it down and put up a new tent. They asked me for my opinion.

I said, "It's costly to do and it will look ugly. And it's not a permanent structure."

They told me to go ahead with my plan for a very large, open-air structure. I did it with the help of my son, Louie. I hired an architect and we started in the fall and finished by spring—in time for golf season. We did it under time and under budget. It's a beautiful addition to the club—it combines the outdoors with a huge roof. It's the best of two worlds. Two years later, I'm still getting compliments from the members.

Besides sports like golf and tennis, I also enjoy a good game of gin or pinochle. Back in my young days, there were three really close friends that I would socialize with: Louie Racine, Joe Farina and Tony Salase.

We began to play pinochle every Wednesday night, come hell or high water. We took turns about whose house to play in. We would start at 6:00 P.M. and would go to 11:00 P.M. At that time our wives would have a nice snack for us and then we would continue to play.

I can tell you these were very tense games. I remember one time my partner made a big mistake and I got up and took the metal chair that I was sitting on and I banged it on the cellar floor. It bounced and hit the ceiling!

This was at the house of another friend, Oscar LiDonni, and he wasn't happy at all; in fact, three days later he sent me an invoice to have the ceiling fixed. He meant it as a joke—but still.

Another time, we were playing at Tony Salase's house in Weston. He had a big playroom with knotty-pine walls. Again, I got upset and threw the cards against the wall. We went to retrieve the cards so that we could complete the game, but we couldn't find two cards. So I went into my car and took out a pinch bar and I started to take down the new knotty-pine. I never heard anybody screaming so loudly! Tony woke up his whole family. But, guess what? I found the two cards behind the knotty pine and we finished our game.

Then, another night, we were playing in my house and I got upset with my partner and I got up and said that I was going home. When I went upstairs I realized that I already was home; I had no option but to go back downstairs and finish the game.

Once, we were playing at Joe Farina's house and his wife Peggy was ready to give birth—she was having labor pains. Joe kept saying to her, "One more game." This went on for some time and finally her water broke and she said, "We need to go now!" Joe replied, "Let me finish this hand." Finally, he took Peggy to the hospital; he said afterwards that it didn't take long for the baby to come.

This kind of craziness went on every week—and I could easily tell you more stories.

But, guess what? At the end of each night, we paid off our losses, shook hands and would leave, looking forward to the next week's game. Having something to do like that on a regular basis is a great boost to your morale.

I think this would be a good place to mention my adventure with motor boating. Or misadventure—perhaps.

It was in the spring of 1965. As I've said, I was a pretty good golfer, even though I only took it up in my late 30s. Like everything else, I worked hard and played hard.

However, this particular spring, lots of things were happening to me, so my mind was not consistently on my golf game, and I was playing really badly with my regular Sunday-morning foursome. Of course I was not happy. On top of my poor play, my friends were giving me a hard time, which I fully understood since I did the same to them.

The worst thing happened on the 12th hole at Oakley Country Club. It's a short par three, no more than 130 yards long, but very tight. When I hit my tee shot it went out of bounds. I took another shot and not only did it go out of bounds—it went onto the tennis courts! I got so upset that I took all the clubs out of my golf bag and I broke every one over my knees—and the golf bag went into the trash barrel. I walked back to the clubhouse, I cleaned out my locker and I paid off my losings to my friends and went home. I told my wife that I was done with golf, and of course she laughed at me.

But I stayed away from golf. I began to spend more time around the house, building patios, walks and gardens. I also spent more time with the kids.

BUILDING MY LIFE

At the same time I kept my membership at Oakley and we continued to meet and socialize with our friends. Everyone was taking bets that I would return soon, but, no, I had made up my mind and I wanted to do some things around the house and spend more time with my family. However, I was driving my wife crazy. She begged me to go back and play golf. But, instead, I decided to look into boating.

There was a sailing school going on in the Boston Harbor, and Susanne, Michael and I signed up for sailing lessons. We really had a wonderful time. However, sailing was too slow. I needed horsepower.

We had planned to take a vacation on Cape Cod that summer since my mother owned a home at Popponesset, and I thought I would buy a small boat so we could do lots of water skiing with the kids.

So here it goes.

Ten days before our trip to the Cape, I bought a 16-foot Chris Craft with a very strong motor that could easily pull two skiers. My brother Jerry also decided to spend the week with us and we made a plan that I would take the boat with the children down by water and he would drive down and meet us at my mother's house.

That morning I called the boat people and told them to gas up the boat and put the boat on the water. So I and my young children, along with my nephew Bobby, who was my brother Jerry's son, all jumped in the boat and off we went on our fun trip.

But it didn't turn out to be fun, because I was not familiar with Boston Harbor and I didn't realize how big it was. In fact, it took us over two hours to find the way out. Which we finally did, but in the meantime we stayed close to the shoreline since this was my very first time out in a boat.

I had not taken any lessons about reading charts—or about what to do or not to do on the water. We were having a good time but, it was getting late in the afternoon. I told "Captain" Bobby Franchi to take over steering the boat, while I concentrated on where we were going. We were getting close to the Cape Cod Canal when all of a sudden I heard a thump. A very loud thump. I looked back and I saw a piece of 4-by-4, about 4-to-6 feet long, that we had hit. At the same time, the motor stalled and I couldn't get it started again and we were drifting away from the land very quickly. It was getting really dark and, of course, there were no cell phones at that time.

Thank God we saw a fisherman. He was far way but he heard us because we were yelling and screaming very loudly and trying hard to signal him. Finally, he came up to us and towed us to a marina in the canal.

At the same time, my brother and my wife were calling the Coast Guard and the local police.

Once we reached the marina, I called my wife at my mother's house. They were relieved that we were safe, and my brother drove to pick us up.

The next morning I called the marina to find out what had happened to the motor. They said that when I hit the 4-by-4, it cracked the shell of the motor and therefore the motor was not able to be repaired. They recommended that I purchase a new motor. I told them to go ahead and get me a new motor.

Welcome to boating!

While waiting for the new motor to arrive, I rented a boat so we could do some water skiing. The boat they gave us was leaking pretty badly, so I took it back and exchanged it for another one. Finally, we were on the water again and we had fun water skiing.

Then my brother Jerry suggested we do some fishing.

One early morning, he and I went fishing, but as we started heading out, the boat stopped. Here we go again! But this time the engine was working. I jumped in the water and I saw that the propeller was not spinning. What happened was that the pin that held the propeller in the motor shaft had broken off. I had no other choice but to tie a rope onto the boat and then around my shoulders, and, walking and swimming through the water, I towed the boat back to shore. Things were not looking good—but then I found an old board on the ground which had nails stuck into it. I pulled a couple out of the wood and used one to replace the pin that had broken. It worked. Jerry and I went back fishing.

The vacation came to an end and my new motor had finally arrived. Two weeks later I decided to have the boat taken by land to the Boston Marina.

The next year, I went to the Boston Boat Show and guess what? I decided to purchase a *larger* boat! After all, I had learned how to get out of the harbor, and I had completed some navigation classes. I also thought I'd like a large boat better because we could enjoy it more as a family.

I bought a 36-foot fishing boat with all the bells and whistles. It would sleep six people and it had a complete kitchen—or galley as boat people say.

As a family, we began to spend lots of time together on the ocean, traveling from one island to another. We looked forward on weekends to going out on "Malinda"—which is what we named the boat, after the first two letters of my wife Madeline's name, together with my daughter Linda's name.

One weekend we decided to go to Martha's Vineyard. I checked the weather and everything looked good. It was indeed good—until we were at the end of the Cape Cod Canal and we hit some really bad weather. My four daughters were sunning on the front deck; Madeline was sitting next to me on the bridge, holding Louie, since he was a baby at the time.

The waves became really uncontrollable—so much so that I thought I was going to lose one of my children overboard. It was that rough. It wouldn't have taken much for a huge wave to knock one of the girls into the ocean.

Then, I saw Patty flying high in the air and she landed awkwardly on her foot and screamed really loudly. I asked Madeline to please hold the wheel—as well as hold the baby—and I went down and brought the girls into the cabin.

All of a sudden we had found ourselves in a very threatening situation. We were really scared. It makes you realize how serious the water can be—how very prepared you have to be.

The boat was under control and the children were safe; but poor Patty was in deep pain. When we reached Martha's Vineyard, I took her to the local hospital and they x-rayed her and it turned out that she had a broken ankle. Luckily there was an orthopedic surgeon from New England Baptist Hospital who was on vacation and he operated on Patty. We had to leave Patty in the hospital there while we took the boat back home. Then my wife went back and got Patty and then took her to New England Baptist Hospital where she had to stay for a few days until she could come home.

What a weekend!

Then there was the time that a few friends and I decided to go tuna fishing. One of the guests was a young attorney who had just joined our company; his name was Dick Saletta. He wanted to come, but he said he had to be sure we would be back before 7:00 P.M. because he was engaged to be married and he and his parents were to meet for dinner with his future in-laws. I said it would be no problem—because my boat had twin inboard motors and we would easily get back by 7:00 P.M.. Guess what? On our way back, one of the motors caught on fire! So we had only one motor left to take us home. Dick never made the 7:00 P.M. dinner, but he did eventually marry that young lady and they are very happy with a lovely family. So it ended up all right.

On my next ocean episode, four golf buddies and I planned to take a weekend boat trip to Cape Cod and explore the area. We picked a date to go, which was a Friday after work. The day before, I stocked the boat with food and liquor and gassed her up—to make sure everything was set to go and we wouldn't lose any time on Friday afternoon. On the way to the Boston marina, I heard the weather report, which was not favorable for ocean travel. When I reached the marina my buddies were waiting for me and I noticed that a red flag was flying—which indicated hurricane conditions.

But, since we had planned this trip for such a long time, we decided to go!

My friends at the marina tried to talk me out of it, but off we went. As we motored out of the harbor, the waves got bigger and bigger. It was so bad that the waves were going over our heads on the bridge area. We all had put our life jackets on, and two of my friends went down into the cabin and started sipping on a bottle of Scotch and said if we were going down they didn't want to feel any pain! Before I knew it, I was left alone on the bridge. Going through the Canal was bad but at the end of the Canal the sea was very rough. The boat was really swaying from one side to the other. I was able to touch the sea with my hand! We never saw another motor or sail boat during our trip. Once we reached the marina at Falmouth, where I had made reservations for a slip, it took me three or four attempts to come close to the slip. I got help from the marina employees and we were able to tie the boat to the dock

There we were. We showered and went out for a good steak dinner. This was around 9:30 P.M. We sat in a booth and we had a couple of drinks. But when the dinners came, we had a very hard time trying to cut the meat because our bodies were still swaying from side to side!

Anyway, we returned to our boat and went to sleep. Early the next morning we heard people knocking on our door—and guess who they were? My buddies' wives! Yes, my buddies' wives had driven to Falmouth to "rescue" their husbands. We had breakfast and they took off.

I was left alone. I started my trip back home all by myself. But it was really a pleasure, because the storm had gone away and the ocean was calm, like a sheet of glass.

My wife and I and our family and friends took a few more trips on our boat. Finally, I decided that it was time to sell the boat and go back to playing golf.

They say your two happiest days when you own a boat are the day you buy the boat and the day you sell the boat.

They are very right.

Let me finish this chapter by saying that as much as I love playing sports—and all kinds of games—I don't spend a lot of time watching sports.

I used to. But over the years I guess I've been jaded by all the money. And all the issues with drugs. And all the issues with crime.

Maybe sports were always tainted by those things and we just never heard about them.

It galls me to see players charging for their autographs.

It bothers me to see baseball players, who make twenty or thirty times more money than Ted Williams or Mickey Mantle or Babe Ruth ever did in their careers, complaining about money and complaining about petty injuries and not giving their all in every game they play.

We all have off days.

But most of us give it our best, most of the time.

I think a lot of professional athletes don't set good examples for kids. I wish pro players would pay as much attention to American kids as they do to the American dollar.

CHAPTER TWENTY-THREE
Fran

In an odd sort of way, I wouldn't have met Fran if it weren't for Jill. Several years after Madeline passed away, I met a woman in Florida. Her name was Jill. She was divorced and had two grown children. Jill and I started dating. It was nice to have someone to share time with.

After many dates in Florida, we decided to get married. Jill's daughter and I didn't get along; I thought she was conniving. But I have nothing but the greatest respect for Jill's son. Because, a while before the wedding, he talked with me and asked, "Are you sure you want to marry my mother right now? Maybe you should date her longer?"

Looking back, I realize I should have heeded his admonition. But Jill and I were married, and after four short months I realized that this wasn't going to work. Jill and I were divorced and she went back to Florida to live.

But, while Jill was up here in Massachusetts, she and I played in the Charles River Country Club's "Couples Cup" tournament. In the finals, we faced Fran and her partner.

So, after the divorce, I kept seeing Fran at the club. It took a while —I've said that I'm very shy—but I eventually asked her out.

She turned me down.

"Why?" I asked.

"What the hell," she said, "you're married!"

I explained that I was no longer married and she agreed to go out with me.

That was twenty-four years ago.

Fran is very thoughtful, very intelligent, very caring. She's family oriented and she threw herself into my family and embraced my children. In return, they love her and rely on her quite a bit for advice and guidance.

Fran and I live in separate homes—which may or may not be the basis for a great relationship. I'm not sure about that. I just know that we have a great relationship.

Fran has a lot of interests, but cooking isn't one of them. A while ago, she said she was going to have her whole kitchen done over and I asked, "Why would you do that? You never use it!"

That probably wasn't smart.

She got the new kitchen, complete with all top-of-the-line appliances, including a great stove and oven. She never, as far as I can tell, uses the oven. Except—as I've said—when she bakes birthday cakes for my children and grandchildren, which she does for each and every birthday. So, I guess the new kitchen was a good idea after all.

Probably the biggest thing Fran and I do is travel.

I've always loved traveling, and Fran and I have been fortunate to take a number of great trips together.

Our first trip was to Italy. We stayed for two-and-a-half weeks and had the best time ever.

We flew into Sicily, and stayed in a nice small hotel in downtown Palermo; we mixed with the real people—the local people. After two days there, we rented an automobile and started our journey toward

Catania, a large city, the second-largest on Sicily, on the east coast of the island, facing the Ionian Sea.

Our first stop was at some old ruins—I can't remember the name—but they are very well known. Then we went to Taormina, a small town at the bottom of a mountain, facing the sea. The beach was wonderful and the town was very picturesque. It had beautiful outdoor restaurants and coffee shops and lots of bottegas—which are small shops. And they had a great Roman open-air theater which presented entertainment every afternoon and evening. I could have spent a whole week there, and I'd strongly recommend it to anyone visiting Sicily.

The trip was great, but Fran was not happy with my driving. Every time I would pass a vehicle or take a sharp turn she would yell, "Oh, Jesus!" This went on for the next two weeks. At one point I thought I *was* Jesus. We finally reached Catania, and from there we took a ferryboat to the mainland, to Calabria, the region in southern Italy located at the "toe" of the peninsula. From there we began our trip north.

We had no hotel reservations, so we stayed wherever it pleased us.

We drove along the Amalfi Coast—which, to Fran's horror, is a very narrow highway along the side of a mountain with no guard rails! We'd be looking down about three to four hundred feet to the ocean. It was beautiful, but a bit scary and I heard "Oh, Jesus!" about a thousand times.

We finally reached Sorrento, and Fran ran for the first bar! She fell in love with their famous drink, limoncello.

From Sorrento we took a boat to the island of Capri and then once back on the mainland we drove to Naples. Then we visited the ruins of Pompeii.

After that visit, we drove to Rome. The Eternal City. We stayed in Rome for three or four days and then hit the road again.

We went to Monte Cassino, where the horrible, hard-fought battle of World War II was fought in early 1944.

After that, we drove to Atina—this is the town that my society that had the bocce club was named after.

And we went to my home of Gallinaro. It was wonderful to show Gallinaro to Fran, the house where I was born and our farm and the countryside. And, of course, the well and the fig trees!

From there we drove to Florence. Again, we had no hotel reservations. To make matters worse, there was a big celebration going on.

We looked for an hour-and-a-half for a hotel and finally found a very noisy place where couples came and left every two hours. We got out of that joint early the next morning and found a real hotel. We loved Florence.

From there, we drove to Venice, where, believe it or not, we stayed at a five-star hotel on the waterfront. What a difference between that hotel and the first hotel we had in Florence! But we can say that we saw it all—from five stars to stars of ill repute.

Our final stop was Milan. Milan is more of a business, industrial city. We had always been told to watch out for gypsy people—who I had never encountered in all my other trips to Italy. Sure enough, Fran and I were walking through a mall and a gypsy family surrounded us, asking for money. They were getting quite nasty. Thank God that a bunch of locals came and rescued us.

We finally boarded our plane and flew home—sweet home.

It's nice to travel, but it's nice to enter your own home again.

Our next trip was a little farther away—Australia. Another wonderful trip. Neither of us had ever been there, but we'd heard so much about it. It is truly a beautiful and big country. The people were very warm. The food and lodging was great.

And the golf courses were magnificent. Especially since I was able to beat Fran—but I'm still waiting for her to pay our bet!

We drove through the outback and met aboriginal people. And we had a great cookout with the locals.

From there we drove to a resort which was near the Great Barrier Reef. We dove into the ocean there and saw all the outstanding coral formations.

We went to New Zealand and took a bus ride to see the sights. We saw sheep—lots of sheep. Huge numbers of sheep. We took a boat ride and saw almost as many dolphins as we had seen sheep. New Zealand is a wonderful country, lots of open space and very, very nice people.

On our way home, we took a side trip to the small island of Fiji. Another perfect spot. Good beaches, good weather, good people. Another great golf course—and, again, I'm still waiting for my winnings.

It's funny—when she wins, which isn't that often, she puts her hand out and keeps looking at me for the payoff.

But when she loses, she'll say, "Tomorrow, tomorrow."

And guess what? I'm still waiting.

Finally, we flew home. It was a fantastic trip, but I don't think I'd do it again because of how very long the flights are.

On all of our trips, we usually try to play golf. We've played golf in Italy, Australia, New Zealand, Fiji, Spain, Ireland and Scotland. Probably some other places I can't remember.

In Scotland, we played at the historic and storied St. Andrews. Which is a very different experience. The fairways are very dry, which makes them very fast. The roughs have tall grass. Hit a ball in there and it's gone. The course isn't at all flat; it's full of many rolling hills. A very beautiful spot.

Needless to say, I'm still waiting for my winnings!

Our trip to Spain was adventuresome. We flew into Madrid and then rented a car—with me driving and Fran trying not to flinch. We went to Barcelona where we saw the very beautiful Basilica of the Holy Family, which is a twentieth-century church designed by the renowned Spanish architect Antoni Gaudi.

We also saw the site of the Barcelona Olympic Stadium which hosted the 1992 games. Very impressive. That was the Olympics where the flame was lit by an archer shooting a flaming arrow over the cauldron which lit the gas.

We continued on to Lisbon, which we thoroughly enjoyed. We played golf at the very beautiful Don Pietro Country Club in Costa Del Sol. Needless to say—winnings?

We continued driving, with Seville as our next goal. It was late afternoon and I was driving and Fran was navigating with a map. It was raining hard—it was raining horizontally. When we realized that we had driven over the same bridge four times, I decided to stop and ask someone for assistance. We were only a block away! So we got there and went inside and the clerk at the registration desk said that they had the reservation, but that it was only for Fran.

The person behind the counter said to me, "You can't stay."

"If I can't stay, she's not staying," I replied.

Well, he relented. I have never had any idea what that was all about.

But we were so tired and so glad to have a room at last that we slept very soundly.

Venice aside, we generally don't go in for five-star hotels. As long as it's clean and is in a good location, that's all that matters to us.

I usually made the reservations, but in one town in Spain Fran had picked the hotel. It was fine, except the only way to turn the lights on or off in the room was to clap your hands! We thought that was so funny.

"At least the hotels I pick have light switches," I said to Fran. "You don't have to clap your hands."

We had lots of laughs and we still laugh when we talk about it.

From Seville we drove into Portugal.

I don't like to plan trips too much. I'm a bit of an open-road sort of guy. But we would call ahead to make hotel reservations when possible.

In Portugal, we got a little tired of eating in restaurants, so one day we went to a little store and bought some good red wine and fresh-baked bread and cheese and prosciutto.

We found a nice spot by the ocean and had a great picnic. These are the things you remember.

BUILDING MY LIFE

We also drove to Gibraltar—to the coast—which is breathtaking. We were at the top of a mountain looking out over the sea. Then we saw Barbary Macaques–those little monkeys with the piercing green eyes. They are endangered but are thriving in Gibraltar. We got very close to them. One of the little guys ran right up to Fran and tried to eat her ham sandwich! Then he tried to swipe her pocketbook. Fran loved it. She kept shooing him away—but she didn't mind at all when he came back. It was a fun afternoon.

Oh, I remember that we also played golf in Portugal. Once again—winnings? Still waiting.

The next big trip was to Egypt. That was exciting. We flew into Cairo and then we booked a boat trip down the Nile. It's simply another world. The sights, the water, the land, the ruins. It's ancient history right there in front of you.

One day, the boat pulled up at a little village and we went shopping. Fran saw a store that sold leather goods and she wanted to buy a pocketbook.

So, we went inside and began looking at stuff.

It was summer; Fran was wearing shorts. She's very attractive and very athletic. She was noticed by the man who owned the store.

He came up to me and, right in front of Fran, he said to me in English, "How many camels would you take for her?"

I was speechless. Well, for a moment.

"Make me an offer," I finally said to him.

He made his offer: "Four camels."

"No," I answered, "at least six camels per leg."

The man came right back with a new offer of six total camels.

"Twelve," I said.

This went on for a while.

Fran looked at us—not knowing what in the world to think. She's a good sport and took it all in fun.

Although I did miss a chance to own some camels, I can't really fault the guy. Fran does have great legs.

A very different kind of trip was a riverboat ride that started in Amsterdam. It lasted two weeks. We went through the Netherlands, Germany, Austria and Hungary. We'd stop all the time at nice, quaint villages. The people were charming. And we got to see the home of Mozart.

Finally, let me tell you about our most recent trip.

Normandy.

The beaches of D-Day.

Fran and I went in October of 2013. What a trip!

It's overwhelming. When you stand on the beaches and look out at the ocean and think back to June 6, 1944. I was just sixteen years old and still in trade school back in Newton. But, of course, I remember it happening and I remember people talking about it and the newspapers and the radio reporting on it.

Referred to as Operation Overlord, and under the command of General Dwight D. Eisenhower, D-Day was the most momentous invasion in the history of mankind. The Allied forces landed on the beaches of Normandy and breached the Nazis' supposedly unbreachable Atlantic Wall—a long row of fortifications stretching all along the French coastline that the Germans thought was impregnable.

They were wrong.

BUILDING MY LIFE

It was the beginning of the end for the Third Reich. It was the beginning of the end for Nazi Germany. It was the beginning of the end for tyranny and evil and oppression.

At 6:30 A.M., on June 6, 1944, one hundred and fifty thousand American, English and Canadian soldiers rode flat-bottomed landing craft through the choppy seas of the English Channel as close to the shore as they could. They were aiming for five sections of beach, code named: Sword, Juno, Gold. Omaha and Utah. And when the ramps went down, these unbelievably brave young men jumped into the water as enemy machine guns opened up from all directions in front of them. The German guns were pre-aimed and were positioned so that they would shoot at angles to each other, creating a deadly crossfire.

And those men sloshed their way toward the shore. And those men ran and stumbled and crawled and inched their way forward.

More than five thousand of those men would not survive the next few hours. The stories of what they did can fill a library. It is the story of freedom.

And there I was, standing on the sand of Omaha Beach.

It was monumental.

We took a tour and it turned out that I was the only veteran. The tour guide contacted CNN and they called to interview me, but, unfortunately, Fran and I were already in Paris by the time they called, so I never made it to TV.

In a way, I'm glad. Sure I served in the Marines; but I wasn't one of the men who charged down a ramp into the ocean surf and fought my way toward the beach. I probably would have said something foolish. But if anyone reads this, let me say that we owe those men who did rush down the ramps so very much. It's no exaggeration to say that we owe those men everything we have.

We stayed at a very nice, very quaint inn in the village of Bayeux; only a short distance from the beaches. It was a great place. But—the French aren't going to like this—the food was terrible. I mean really terrible.

Food aside, my only regret is that we couldn't see the American cemeteries as well as the other cemeteries of the Allied dead. Because of the crisis in the U.S. Congress over the budget, President Obama had ordered that many federally operated facilities had to temporarily close. We went to the cemeteries, but the gates were closed. Regardless, what we did see from a distance was still awe-inspiring.

In the village of Sainte-Mère-Église there is a very striking image. During D-Day, an American paratrooper was landing when his chute got tangled in the steeple of a church. He couldn't get down. He was up there, dangling, for hours.

The Germans didn't shoot him because they thought he was dead. He was eventually captured, but then managed to escape. What a story! So, as a memorial, today there is a dummy paratrooper hanging by a tangled chute up in the steeple of the church. You just look up and wonder about it all.

I thought it was gratifying to see that the French are so indebted to Americans for what we did to free them. The French maintain the cemeteries and the beaches; they've put up a lot of little monuments and memorials all over the place—both to commemorate what happened and to explain it to tourists.

As for me, I never walked so much in my life!

All around Normandy. The beaches. The villages.

Then Fran and I went to Paris. We walked from morning until night. We saw a million things.

We both loved the Eiffel Tower, which was built in 1889 as the entrance to the World's Fair. We went to the top and looked at all of Paris beneath us.

The Louvre was breathtaking—even before you go inside! It's an amazing building—with that modern glass pyramid in the courtyard. Originally built as a palace for the king, it was officially opened as a museum in 1793. Just think—in 1793 in the United States, George Washington was finishing his first term as president!

The Arc de Triomphe, the classic monument to those who fought and died for France in the French Revolution and in the Napoleonic Wars, which is also the home for France's tomb of the unknown soldier, is very moving. Very elegant. It's a massive structure—with people and traffic moving around it and through it.

The Cathedral of Notre Dame was an inspiration. Originally built in 1160—think of that, 1160!—it's been changed and remodeled and rebuilt over the centuries. It was one of the first buildings in the world to use flying buttresses.

I never built anything with a flying buttress. Maybe I should look into it. Anyway, I got a wonderful souvenir gold coin at Notre Dame that I'll always keep on me as a good-luck charm.

So we walked and we walked and we walked. I walked poor Fran nearly to death. She was upset with me one day, when I sort of tricked her into going to one more place before we went back to our hotel. I think her legs hurt more than mine. Of course, as the Egyptian shopkeeper will attest, her legs are also a lot better looking than mine.

The traffic! People think Boston traffic is crazy? I've been to Rome and I thought traffic there was nuts. But nothing—nothing—compares to traffic in Paris! I have driven all my life—and I've driven in many countries around the world. But I've never seen anything like that. We mostly walked—once we took a cab—so at least I didn't have to listen to Fran complaining about my driving! That one cab driver really had us on our toes. Not because of the speed, but because of his desire to fight other drivers to make a turn. I really thought he was going to have an accident. But, nothing happened.

Oh, the food in Paris wasn't any better than the food in Normandy. All you hear about is French cuisine. We didn't like any of it!

And it's not like we've never been out of our own backyard. We've traveled all over the world. We've eaten in more countries than most people. And we've eaten all kinds of unusual food.

We just didn't like French food. Fran would try some different dishes, but I like simple things and just didn't like what we were served.

Thankfully, I found a good Italian restaurant in Paris. We ate all of our meals there for the rest of the trip.

We left Paris for a side trip to Versailles.

When you see Versailles, you know why the French people revolted.

What an incredible amount of money was spent on the palace and the grounds—while peasants were starving! It's opulence beyond imagination.

But, looking at the giant edifice, I did say to myself, "I could build this."

Sure it's got 700 rooms—and 2,153 windows—and 67 staircases—and covers 563,000 square feet. Sure there are 12 miles of enclosing walls, 50 fountains and 21 miles of water conduits.

Big deal. We could build that.

It's funny how different people see things differently. Fran notices the beauty, the art, the history.

I notice how it must have been built.

Looking up at the Eiffel Tower, I thought to myself that if I built a launch tower for the Mercury space program, then I could build this. Basically, it's a giant Erector Set. I did marvel how they built it back then; they didn't have sophisticated scaffolding like we have today. Instead of welding, like we did at Cape Canaveral, they put the tower together with rivets. They heated the rivets and then tossed them up to the workers! A worker would catch the rivet in a bucket and then put it in place and hammer it. In a way, it was like building Tunis University, where we had to do just about everything by hand. Many of the techniques we had to use in Tunisia were less advanced than the techniques they used in Paris to build the Eiffel Tower.

I see buildings all over the world in the same way—from a builder's perspective.

In Rome, when we visit St. Peter's, I marvel at how they built that amazing structure without heavy equipment. The stones had to be carried by cart from miles away, on skids, pulled by horses. Not too much different, when I think about it, from my father carting stones to build my mother a well.

I've been to St. Peter's a number of times. On one trip, I had taken my young daughter Susanne with me and I hired a private tour guide to take her around. I couldn't help lingering nearby and listening in! At one point, I stepped forward and asked him a question about the giant pillars that were being repaired.

"Mr. Franchi," he said, "I'm here every day, and I've never paid attention to that at all."

It's like anything. Sometimes you can be too close to notice.

If you work in construction, it's in your blood.

I admired all the work that was done in Rome—for St. Peter's, the Colosseum and countless other marvels.

Think of all the laborers, a lot of them were slaves, working day in and day out. In some cases, the work wasn't completed for a hundred years. So you could go to work, knowing that some day your great-grandchildren would finish the job.

I couldn't function like that.

I'm too much the driven American.

I have to know it's going to be finished—by me!

I am rewarded by seeing the job done—by seeing all my effort result in something that has value and that will serve people for years and years to come.

BUILDING MY LIFE

CHAPTER TWENTY-FOUR
Yahoo! This is fun!

When I lost my children to cancer—when I went through that experience—I saw that the sick child, quite naturally, got all the attention. The strain on the other children was terrible, but there wasn't much that could be done. Fighting cancer is a full-time job.

I know. I've been there. My family has been there. I didn't see anything that could be done about it. After all, like I've said, cancer doesn't just attack a person, cancer attacks the entire family.

Then I got an idea.

As the owner of Wildcat Mountain Ski Resort, I realized that I had the opportunity to give something back to families who had kids who were sick from cancer.

I knew what the experience of a sick child can do to a family. So I decided to bring up whole families, parents and all children, all expenses paid, for a long weekend of skiing and fun at Wildcat. I went to Dana-Farber and they thought it was a great idea.

So we held our first Yahoo Weekend.

We started with fifty families—with all their children. They all came and they all had a really great time. Most importantly—for a brief time at least—they forgot some of their problems. They were still a family who had a child sick with cancer. But, for a little time at least, they were simply a family having fun.

We do this trip over the Patriot's Day weekend each spring, because it's four days and the weather is warmer which makes it easier for all the kids, especially the sick ones—who range from two to fourteen years old.

When they arrive each year, the mountain belongs to them!

Fran and I go to every Yahoo Weekend, of course. As do my children and many of my grandchildren. Everyone participates and helps out.

And all of the mountain staff donates their time to help out.

At the ski school, our staff outfits all the kids with skis and boots. Putting on all those boots isn't easy! But they do it.

For children who can't ski, we have all kinds of other activities—like clowns and face painting. We also take them for a ride up to the top of the mountain on the chair lift, and we give them ski-mobile rides—and just lots of other things along the course of the long weekend.

Sometimes we've had less than 50 families—because a child got very sick and the family had to cancel. That's always very sad.

But overall it's been successful. It's been one of the best things I've ever done. To see children who are so sick—and who want to participate, who want to have fun—it's all so wonderful and all so sad at the same time.

And we're about to have our twenty-fifth year! Each year with fifty families coming up for all the fun.

If we don't see repeat children, that's good news. My goal is to never see the family back the next year, because that would indicate that the child's cancer is in remission. And that is great news.

Even after I sold Wildcat, I put in the provision that I would be able to do Yahoo each year as long as I'm living.

Oh, the name. Let me explain that.

That happened by chance. On the Saturday night of each weekend we have a big banquet for everyone, and there are speeches.

At the first banquet, I was talking and asking if they were having a good time. You know how it goes. They'd say something, and I'd say something like, "I can't hear you."

And then I just shouted out, "This is a great time. Yahoo! This is fun!"

It was called Yahoo Weekend ever since.

In fact, there is now a Yahoo Room at Dana-Farber, a quiet place for families to rest and talk.

Dana-Farber has been great. They send nurses along to help out with the sick children. A few times, some of the kids got really bad and had to be sent to the hospital. I felt terrible. At least they got to spend some time there with their family.

One year there was no snow. We held it anyway, and we did all kinds of things. Horseback rides. Hay rides. Hikes. We still had a great time.

My job each year is to make certain everything runs smoothly.

But Fran and I also make sure we do one thing that we really enjoy. And that is giving those ski-mobile rides to the kids who couldn't ski. We fly up the mountain! What fun they have. It's great to see all the kids in line, eagerly waiting for their turn. Fran and I enjoy that a lot. It's the highlight of our time with the kids.

We also run a scavenger hunt where the kids have to scour the area for a list of things to find—and they get a prize for their effort at the Saturday-night banquet. Oh, one really great thing that's a lot of fun is that we have a big dance after the banquet. To see all the kids up there dancing away. To join in with them. The music. The smiles. The kids and dance moves. It's the best.

Fran and I just marvel at those kids. You can laugh and cry at the same time. We try to laugh. There's too much crying.

The Yahoo Weekends bring back a lot of memories for me.

I see that no matter what, children are children and have to be themselves.

It's been amazing how many letters and cards and drawings and phone calls I've gotten from kids and siblings and parents—thanking me and my family for giving this little time for them to enjoy together as a family.

That's nice, but they're the ones doing the wonderful thing.

That's why I'll keep doing Yahoo as long as I'm alive.

After that, I'm counting on my family to carry on, especially Louie and Deirdre, who have taken over this responsibility in recent years.

BUILDING MY LIFE

CHAPTER TWENTY-FIVE
Grandpa

I have six children, nine grandchildren, and four great-grandchildren.

I've done of lot of building in my life.

But the legacy I'm proud of is my family.

So let me talk about all these kids in order, so that no one thinks I have a favorite!

My daughter Linda and her husband Jack have four children.

Jennifer is the oldest. She works as the office manager of her father's orthodontist practice. Jennifer is married to Peter Carney and they have four children—my great-grandchildren: Mackenzie, Garrett, Rowan and Jack.

Linda's second child is her son, Michael, who is an orthodontist as well. Michael is very athletic, very lovable, very caring. Michael is married to Amber.

Then there is Laura, who is very smart. She went to Wake Forest University and now works in Rhode Island in the state education administration office. Laura is married to Brian.

And finally there's Kristin, who followed in my footsteps and works for a developer managing apartment complexes. Kristin is married to Elliot.

With Laura's marriage, my daughter Linda claims she is "free." She can now spend more time on the golf course. She deserves it.

Debra and Dean had a little girl named Madeline, after my wife. After Debra passed away, Dean and his sister Barbara raised Madeline.

Madeline really takes after her mother. She went to American University and then to graduate school for art. She's done really well. She's very open minded, ambitious and high spirited. She's an adventurer. She's traveled to South America and stayed in local people's homes. She trades for her room and board by teaching art to young people in the area. She loves to travel. She's very down to earth and very frugal.

Then there's my son Louie and his wife Deirdre. Like Linda and Jack, they also have four children.

Jessica, their first born, is very educated. She has very high tastes. She loves nice things. She takes after my daughter Patricia. She isn't shy about spending money. She's traveled a lot; she's studied in Rome. And, from time to time, I get the bills. Well—that's what grandpas are for, right?

Then came Austin, who's very athletic—he's very good at skiing and football. He was captain of his football team at Saint Sebastian's School. He is now at Providence College.

The third child is Sophia, who's also very athletic and very smart and beautiful. Right now she's at Newton Country Day School of the Sacred Heart, where she does great in sports and at the books.

Finally, there's Martha. She's also at Newton Country Day School of the Sacred Heart, where she does well. Martha is my most easy-going one. She participates in everything. She's very social and just a lovely young lady. She'll do fine in the years to come.

It's great being a grandfather. It's beautiful to see them grow up. I love them. I love being with them. I love when they come to visit and I love when they go home!

That's the difference between being a father and a grandfather.

But you know, you see so much of yourself in your grandchildren. I'll think, "That's what I would say" or "That's so much like Madeline." That's what a legacy is, I guess.

When I'm in a certain mood, a good mood, but a quiet sort of thinking mood, I realize that what Luigi and Giovanna started back in Gallinaro was passed on to me.

And what Madeline and I started with our children has been passed on to our grandchildren. And now to great grandchildren. I'm not taking anything away, of course, from my children's spouses and their parents.

I just like it so much when I see a spark of something in the eyes of one of my grandchildren or great-grandchildren, and I can see a little bit of where that spark came from.

It's all so amazing. It's amazing, when I think of it, that I have nine grandchildren and four great-grandchildren. Each of them has a different perspective on life. And if I can, I try to help with college and trips and things.

But as the family gets bigger, it's difficult to get all of us together. In the old days, you'd just throw the kids in the beach wagon and take off.

I remember one trip to Florida. We got to our hotel really late because of a mechanical problem with our plane, and they had given the rooms away.

Simple. Pile the kids in the car and go find another hotel. The next morning, we realized that Susanne had forgotten her suitcase. Nothing to wear! I took her to a shopping center and it was soon fixed.

As I've said earlier, Debra did the same thing on a ski trip. I had to buy her everything. Even all the ski clothes.

After that, I made the kids line up their suitcases all in row and I checked them off before we drove away to another trip.

Things like that were upsetting for the moment, but they give memories that are always with you.

Life is like that. How many funny stories do we tell—that are about things that weren't funny at all when they happened?

The great thing about being human is that we have the ability to look back and appreciate things in the bigger sense. We can forget the small petty problems—and enjoy the memory of the whole event.

BUILDING MY LIFE

CHAPTER TWENTY-SIX
The Long Way Home

I've thought many times about what would have happened if my father had stayed in Italy. What kind of life would all of us have led?

It's impossible to know, of course. But I still think about it a lot.

We were very lucky that my father decided to buy out his brothers in order to own the whole farm in Gallinaro. In Italy, it was a tough time and my family was better off than most families. So if the farm had been divided among my father and his brothers, there would have been a lot less to go around.

I think I would have left Italy anyway. I would have wanted to have gone somewhere where I could get a better life. There's was always something inside of me. I always knew I wanted to better myself. I wanted a better education and I wanted to go to a country with better opportunities.

I had uncles living in Belgium, so I probably would have gone there if my father had stayed in Italy.

This is going to sound like an old-fashioned story, but I really do remember walking about three-to-five miles each way to school every day in Italy. There was no school bus. I'd go with a bunch of kids from my neighborhood, a bunch of friends. And we walked and walked and walked.

As I've said, my mother made great food. And she would bake bread made out of whole wheat, because we could afford it. Most of my friends had bread made out of corn meal, because it was cheaper and it was what was their families could afford. I had never had corn bread, so I would trade my bread for theirs all the time. That's always stuck in my mind. My father was able to give us more than a lot of our neighbors had—because he was in America, working to better our lives. But on the other hand, we had no father except for short visits he would make. When I finally saw my father when we landed in America, I hardly remembered him.

Here's a thing that sticks in my mind from back then in Italy. One day, we got out of school and we were walking home. A bunch of boys got into a stone fight. They started throwing stones at each other. I was minding my own business—how many times has a kid said that? But I was. I happened to turn around and I got hit right in the eye with a stone.

I went running home. On the way, I met my sister and she took me to my mother. My mother, naturally, was very upset. We went to a clinic—like a small hospital. I got stitches. Everyone made a big deal out of it.

That, of course, had nothing to do with living either in Italy or America. Kids are kids. Stones are stones.

When the time did come to go to America, we went to Naples to take the boat. It was my mother, my sister Maria, my brothers Dominic and Anthony, and me.

The boat was the *Conte di Savoia*—which means "Count of Savoy," with Savoy being a region in France in the Alps that at one time was part of Italy.

Anyway, she was one of the largest ships in the world—814 feet long and 96 feet wide, with a gross tonnage of over 48,000 tons. She carried 2,200 passengers. And—for a big boat—she was fast. Her powerful steam engines drove four propellers and she could reach a speed of 27 knots, which is amazing.

It was quite elegant. There was marble everywhere. High ceilings. Elaborate murals. Statues. Very classic.

Unfortunately, I was the only one in my family who got to see it all because everyone except me got really seasick. I never get seasick.

The funny thing is that the *Conte di Savoia* was fitted with special huge gyroscopes that were supposed to make it the smoothest sailing ship in the world!

Tell that to my mother and brothers and sister!

The trip lasted seven days.

While everyone was sick in the staterocm, I walked all over the ship. We had an assigned table for meals—and I was the only one who sat there for the entire trip.

I made friends with one of the crew, and he showed me all over the boat and let me explore at will.

We finally made it.

But the poor *Conte di Savoia* was sunk by the Allies in World War II. She was eventually raised, but then she was sold for scrap. She deserved a better end.

CHAPTER TWENTY-SEVEN
What Do We Build?

Looking back on it all, I honestly don't have any regrets about what I did in my life.

Regret doesn't mean sorrow. I'll never be free of the sorrow of the beautiful people I've lost.

But I don't regret the decisions I made and the things I tried to do.

My upbringing set the stage, I guess. Because even at a very young age, I always had a good vision of what I wanted my life to be like. I set out to accomplish certain things and I was able to be successful.

I know how fortunate I was in business. I was able to do just about everything I put my mind to. I never demanded things. I never took anything. I did everything with a reason behind it. I always followed my vision.

I do wish that I had had more schooling. Because of my language barrier when I arrived here, I went to trade school. I would have liked to have completed high school—and that would have helped me more with English as well. But, of course, going to trade school got me in the direction of construction—and that turned out to be a very successful path.

Because of the way I feel about school, I have established an education endowment for my grandchildren. I want them to have the opportunity to get as much education as possible, without worrying about how to pay for it. That's one thing I can do for them that I know will serve them well in life. I realize that my parents gave me a lot of advice that I've found useful my whole life—and I want to pass that kind of opportunity on to my grandchildren.

Okay. Here's one regret. If I could live my life over again, I'd like to be a doctor. To see a person who is very sick—and be able to help out—and see that person well again—that would make me feel really good.

That's why I think it's important to help people whenever you can. In any way you can. I've had resources, so I've been able to help a lot of people who needed money or a job or who wanted to start their own business. If everyone tried to help others, with whatever resources one may have, well that would be a happier world.

I think of Italy a lot. I've been there many times over the years, and as soon as I hit the ground in Rome and hear the language it all comes back to me. I can speak pretty well once I'm there, and I know that because the locals don't make fun of me. Not like my brother Tony. They make fun of him all the time. His wife, Connie, is well schooled in Italian. She also gets a kick out of it when Tony tries to speak to the locals. It is kind of funny.

Growing up in America, my parents spoke Italian. But my mother insisted that the children speak English. It's a new country, she'd say, we should abide by American standards. My mother, father and my older brothers went to night school, because they were too old for regular school. That's how they learned English.

My mother loved it in America. She had had a hard time in Italy—raising all of us kids and working on the farm and with her husband away a lot.

America was a walk in the park!

My father was a wonderful man. I never heard him say a bad thing about any person. No matter what, he'd get up every morning and go to work. He'd worked hard to support his family. And when he came home, he sat in a comfortable chair under a shady tree in the back yard and had a glass of beer and smoked his pipe.

He took enormous pride in keeping the yard in great shape, especially the vegetable garden. There was a contest between him and a very close friend as to who would have the first ripe tomato.

Watching my father being so gentle and laid back, I made sure not to hire anyone who smoked a pipe! I think people who smoke pipes are too easy going. I don't want easy-going people working for me. They're great people, but I want very energetic people.

That, of course, is a strange thing to say. My father always worked —but I think that deep down inside he would have preferred to be sitting in a comfortable chair, with a bottle of beer, smoking away on his pipe.

Who's to say?

By contrast, my mother was very aggressive. She wore the pants in the family. She managed the purse strings. She made sure we did our chores and ran our errands.

She had a vision to improve our standard of living in America.

She didn't like it at all that we lived in a rented house. She put her eyes on buying 281 Nevada Street in Newton. My father thought it was too risky, too much of a stretch. But my mother—come hell or high water—knew she would get that house.

She pushed and she pushed finally my father gave in and they bought the house, which made my mother very happy.

Then she decided that we should have a house on the Cape!

He we go again!

My poor father.

He wasn't happy about it—but only because of financial concern. He liked the idea of a Cape house—if we didn't have to worry about paying for it.

But my mother was determined. She scouted and scouted until she found a lot she really liked and she bought land in Popponesset. And then she bought two more lots. My mother could be a steamroller once she got going. Eventually, she built two houses.

And then, and this is really odd, I was constructing a missile site at Otis Air Force Base on the Cape. We were tearing down some houses to make room for the missile site, and my mother got it into her head that I should move one of those houses to her land. And I did!

She was certainly a go-getter—blessed with good vision. Such good vision that she later bought another home next to her original two homes.

I think I got her genes—and her vision.

My mother always claimed that I was her favorite son.

Sometimes you wouldn't think so, because we had a lot of head butting over the years.

But we always ended up loving each other.

So—what do we build? And what do we build with?

Well, I've built with steel and concrete and wood and glass.

I've built air bases and hospitals and universities and homes and apartments and condos and offices and stores and clubs and tennis courts and swimming pools.

I've built a launch pad to send brave men and women out of this world.

I'm proud of all of it.

I always had a vision and I always tried my best to do the best job possible.

But is that what we really build?

Even if everything that I built—starting with a chunk of land and then a drawing and then a blueprint and then a crew and then materials and then a finished edifice that people live in and work in and do what they do in—even if all that lasts for a thousand years—is that what I've built?

Sure.

But all of that can't compare to Madeline, Linda, Debra, Patricia, Susanne, Louie, Michael, Fran, Jennifer, little Michael, Laura, Kristin, little Madeline, Jessica, Austin, Sophia, Martha, Mackenzie, Garrett, Rowan and Jack.

As I close up this story, I would like you to see that, when all is said and done, I know exactly what I built.

I know exactly what I did with my life.

I built a beautiful family.

So let me end right here.

Let me end by saying that you should be yourself. Be honest. Be passionate. Be humble. Fight for what you think is right. And, finally, treat a person like you would like to be treated yourself.

And stay healthy.

Pat Franchi was born in Gallinaro, Italy in 1928. At age 12 he came to America—to Newton, Massachusetts—with his family to start a new life.

Not knowing any English at all, Pat entered public elementary school. He did well. He went to trade school afterwards. Then he joined the Marine Corps. Then he started his own construction company.

Pat's business became an international venture—building hospitals and universities and housing complexes in the United States, North Africa and Lebanon. Franchi Construction also built a significant part of Cape Canaveral—including the launch tower for the Mercury missions.

He married Madeline, the love of his life, and they had six children.

Cancer took Madeline and three of their children.

How he endured and how he kept his family together is a story of love, determination, honor—and vision.

Made in the USA
Charleston, SC
17 July 2014